RELIGION AND MYTH

RELIGION AND MYTH

BY THE

Rev. JAMES MACDONALD

NEGRO UNIVERSITIES PRESS

NEW YORK

Originally published in 1883
by David Nutt Co.

Reprinted 1969 by
Negro Universities Press
A Division of Greenwood Publishing Corp.
New York

SBN 8371-1550-7

PREFACE

THIS volume is an effort to put into popular form a number of facts connected with the religious observances and social customs of African tribes. No attempt is made to treat the subject exhaustively, and those who have made Ethnology a study will find in it little that is absolutely new. But the ordinary reader, who is interested in questions affecting a people slowly emerging from barbarism, may have his sympathies quickened.

When I first began the study of Ethnology it opened to me a new world of thought. Reading Mr. J. G. Frazer's *Golden Bough* last winter, I found it touched so many subjects which long residence in Africa had made familiar to me, that the idea of putting the results of my own observations into permanent form took shape. This has been supplemented by facts gleaned from such authorities as were at hand, and the result is the present volume.

I have, in foot-notes, acknowledged my indebtedness to various authors.

The facts have been gathered chiefly from Mr. Frazer's volumes; Bishop Callaway's *Nursery Tales, Traditions and Histories of the Zulus;* Miss C. G. Gordon-Cumming's *In the New Hebrides;* W. Mannhardt's *Antike Wald-und Feld Kulte* and his other works; Winterbotham's *The Niger and Laire Tribes;* Rowley's *Africa Unveiled;* Duff Macdonald's *Africana;* Schweinfurth's *The Heart of Africa;* Chalmers' *Tiyo Soga;* Brownlee's MS. notes; Felkin's *Four Tribes of Central Africa;* Ramseyer's and Kühne's *Four Years in Ashantee;* Ashe's *Two Kings of Uganda;* Arnot's *Garanganze;* the missionaries New and Krapf, G. M. Theal, and several others, without whose works my book could not have been written.

Though living "at the back of the north wind," I still feel the African fever; that is to say, the charm which it has to draw back to itself all who have tasted its bitters and sweets.

My object throughout has been to stimulate an interest in African peoples.

If the book serves this purpose, I shall be amply rewarded for the labour bestowed upon it; in the fullest sense a labour of love.

                                          JAMES MACDONALD.

REAY FREE MANSE,
    Christmas, 1892.

CONTENTS

CONTENTS

RELIGION AND MYTH

CHAPTER I

PRIMITIVE MAN AND THE SUPERNATURAL

RELIGION in the widest sense may be defined as man's attitude towards the unseen, and the earliest forms of human thought furnish the clue from which must be traced the development of those great systems of religion that have at different periods been professed by the majority of men. Under the term religion we must include, not only beliefs in unseen spiritual agencies, but numerous customs, superstitions, and myths which have usually been regarded, by both travellers and students, as worthless and degrading, till within a comparatively recent period. Only by taking account of such, and comparing usages common among tribes far removed from the influence of civilisation with survivals in other parts of the world, can we arrive at any definite knowledge regarding the world's earliest systems of thought.

In both ancient Greece and Italy the union of

royal title with priestly functions was common. At
Rome the tradition was, that the sacrificial king had
been appointed to perform sacred functions formerly
belonging to the ruling monarch, after the overthrow
of the ancient dynasty and the expulsion of the
kings.* In republican Athens the second magistrate
of the city was called King, and his wife Queen. The
functions of both were religious.† Other examples
will occur to readers familiar with the classics.
Such traditions and usages leave no doubt but in
very early times kings were not only civil rulers,
but also the priests who offered the sacrifices and
stood between the worshippers and the unseen
world.

The king would thus be revered as the ruler and
father of his people who protected and cared for
them. He would be also alternately feared and
loved as the ghostly intercessor of men, and regarded as himself partaking of the ghostly nature,
for the divinity which hedged a king in those days
was no empty title, but a sober fact. He was regarded as able to bestow or withhold blessings ; to
bring blight and curse, and remove them ; and so,
being above and beyond the control of his subjects,
reverence and fear would easily pass into adoration
and worship. To us this may appear strange, but it
is quite consistent with savage thought. To the
savage African or South Sea Islander the world is
largely, if not exclusively, worked by supernatural
agents, and these act on impulses similar to those
which move and influence men, and with which he

* Livy.   † J. G. Frazer, *Golden Bough.*

is familiar in himself and others. Where the forces of nature are under the control of the king-priest, the worshipper sees no limit to his power and the influence he can exert on the course of nature, or even upon the material universe itself, as when a man's father's spirit shakes the earth because the king hurt his toe. He holds converse with the gods. From them come abundant crops, fecundity, success in war, and kindred blessings, and the king who bestows these is regarded as having the god residing in his own person ; to the savage man he is himself divine.

There is another way by which the idea of a man-god may be reached. In all countries we find traces of a system of thought which attributed to sympathetic magic events which can only happen in the ordinary course of nature, but which are supposed to be produced by will-power through some object. One of the leading principles of this sympathetic magic is, that any effect may be produced by the imitation of it.* Perhaps the most familiar illustration of this is the Highland " Corp Creadh." This consisted, or consists—for it is said the practice is not extinct—of a clay image of the person to be bewitched being made and placed on a door, taken off the hinges, before a large and constantly replenished fire. Sharp thorns, pins and needles, were pushed into it ; oaths and imprecations were uttered over it, the victim writhing in agony the while ; elf arrows were darted against it, and the fire stirred to a blaze as the image was turned and toasted to make the sufferer feel all the torments of the damned.

* J. G. Frazer, *Golden Bough*.

Finally, the " Corp Creadh " was broken to pieces, when the patient died a horrible death, blue flames issuing from his mouth.   In Africa a small bundle, with a charm, tied to a pigeon's leg, keeps the person bewitched nervous and restless as the bird flits from twig to twig.   If no accident happens to the charm or the bird that carries it, there is no hope for the patient's recovery ; he will simply be worried to death.

This magic sympathy goes farther.   It is supposed to exist between a man and any portion of his person that may be severed from the body, as cut nails, hair, saliva, or even the impression left when he sits down on the grass.   The same sympathy exists between persons hunting, fishing, on a journey, or at war, and those left behind.   If those who remain at home break any of the prescribed rules, disaster or failure overtakes those of their friends who are absent.   According to the same superstition, animals, fowls, and crops may be influenced through tufts of hair, feathers, or green leaves of corn as the case may be, and among savages elaborate precautions are taken for their protection and preservation. " Medicine " poured out on the path by which a man usually approaches his dwelling affects him, should he return by that path, as if he had swallowed it.   A hair from a cow's tail steeped in the virus of any disease prevalent among cattle will affect the animal from which it was taken, and through it the herd.   A green leaf of corn scorched against a fire, or placed where it will mildew, will produce drought or blight in the field or district from which it was taken. These are illustrations of the evils that may be produced by sympathetic magic, but it is capable of being applied to good purposes also.

A South African, in calling a village to a hunt, goes from hut to hut imitating the movements of some well-known animal of the chase. The villagers pelt him with cow-dung, which he does his best to avoid. Should he be well bespattered when he has finished his rounds, the hunt will be successful; if not, it will be entered upon in a heartless manner, as all will expect failure. In Niass when a wild pig falls into a snare it is taken out and rubbed with nine fallen leaves, the belief being that this will cause nine other pigs to fall into the pit.* A South Sea Islander when unsuccessful with his nets walks about as if ignorant of their existence, till caught himself, after which he goes home assured of success on the morrow. As a boy, when fishing about Loch Aline, we often, when luck went against us, used to make pretence of throwing one of the fellows over-board and hauling him out of the water. After that trout or sillock began to nibble, according as we were on fresh water or salt. These superstitions are world-wide. Actions are performed or avoided by all peoples because they entail results similar to, or in some way connected with, the action. So it is that a fashionable lady will throw a pinch of salt over her shoulder when any has been spilled.

Another form of this superstition is securing certain desirable qualities of animals or objects

* J. G. Frazer, *Golden Bough.*

for oneself. A Kaffir warrior twines tufts of rat
hair with his own, as this will give him a rat's
chances of escape from the enemy's spears. Bechuanas use ferret-skins for a similar purpose, or it may
be hair from a hornless ox, as being hard to catch
and harder to hold. Thieves in South Africa affect
the skin of the common wild cat, which is hardly
ever caught when making descents on hen-roosts.
There is not a savage who does not believe that he
can influence nature in some direction, or secure
qualities by means of sympathetic magic, and when
any one obtains more than a village reputation for
his gifts and powers, his deification is merely a
question of time or of local accident. He by degrees
ceases to be the receiver of divine communications,
or the medium through which divine power is exercised, for divinity dwells within him ; he is himself
divine, and can by a touch or look, or even a wish,
produce effects which result from divine power only,
and which in their results go vibrating to the
farthest confines of the universe.

The savage ruler who has attained to the honour
of divinity is expected to give such evidence of his
power as his people need for material prosperity
and comfort, but not more than that. Of these,
health and strength, victory in war, fecundity and
abundant crops, may be regarded as the chief
necessities of primitive man. A shrewd ruler might
keep his reputation unimpaired for a lifetime, as
regards both health and success in battle among a
hardy race of people, nor would he be very much
troubled by those desirous of issue in a land the

inhabitants of which are notoriously prolific.   But the question of crops in seasons of drought, or when there is too great a rainfall, complicates the situation considerably.   And when to these are added hailstorms, tornadoes, insect plagues, and the occasional frosts of tropical lands, it becomes manifest that the divine king sits on an uncertain throne, for all these phenomena he must direct and control for the benefit of himself and his people.

When the sky, for example, indicates the approach of a tornado accompanied by hail, the magician repairs to an eminence, where he collects as many people as can be hastily summoned to his assistance.   These, under his direction and guidance, shout and bellow in imitation of the wind, when with hurricane force it swirls and eddies round the houses and among the forest trees.   Then at a signal they imitate the crash of the thunder, after which there is a dead silence for a few seconds ; then another screech, more piercing and long-continued than any that preceded, dying away in a tremulous wail.   The priest fills his mouth with his own urine, which he squirts in defiant jets against the approaching storm, as a kind of menace or challenge to the wind spirit, the shouting and wailing being intended to frighten the storm spirit from approaching those who resist it.   This is continued till the tornado bursts or passes away in another direction.   In the former case more powerful magic sent it on the course it took ; nothing more could have been done to avert it.   This belongs to a more developed system of thought after the offices of

ruler and priest have been separated. I have
scores of times watched South African magicians
fighting the storm, and when successful the tone of
proud arrogance assumed by the priest was most
amusing, especially to those who did not believe in
his power, and who at times included his own
patron and chief.

This same belief in regard to the power of man to
influence the wind by means of magic is found in
all parts of the world. The Yakut takes a stone,
found inside an animal or fish, and ties it to a stick
with a horsehair. This he waves again and again
round his head, and a cool breeze springs up.* The
New Briton throws burned lime into the air when
he wishes to make wind. Highland witches sold wind
to credulous skippers in knots : one knot opened and
a gentle wind blew ; a second brought a snoring
breeze ; the third a full gale. A simple method of
raising wind to retard the progress of a vessel was
to draw the cat through the fire.† How it came to
be supposed that the suffering of poor pussy had an
effect on the wind the author quoted failed to ascertain. It is well known that a cat scratching table
or chair legs is raising wind, and I once heard a
Scotch matron order her daughter to "drive out
that beast : do ye no see she's making wind, and
we'll no get a wisp o' hay hame the day gin she
goes on." Our Highland friends, too, could sink a
ship at sea by placing an egg-shell in a tub of
water and raising tiny wavelets to sink it. By
sympathy the doomed ship sank.

* J. G. Frazer, *Golden Bough.*   † A. Polson, *Gaelic Society Memoirs.*

Mariners the world over whistle for wind—by courtesy to Neptune in modern times ; formerly, as an act or exercise of power. I tried it once but that was long ago—I am wiser now—and did raise wind ; a hurricane of it, but it was from the skipper, who cursed me by all the gods he knew, and a good many he did not know, for " interfering with what ye know nothing about." The fear of that man has haunted me ever since. Hottentots cause the wind to drop by hanging a fat skin on a pole. The Kaffir raises it by exposing his posterior to the clouds. An Austrian during a storm will open his window and throw out a handful of meal, saying : "There, that's for you : stop."* Wind-bound fisher-men in the Western Isles of Scotland believe that walking sunwise round the Chapel of Fladda, and pouring water on a particular stone, will bring a favourable breeze. If a mariner in the same region ties knots on a cow-hair tether, he may venture to sea, even during a violent gale, as he can, by means of his tether and knots, control the wind at will. Bedouins of East Africa go out to make war on the desert whirlwind, and drive their weapons into the dusty column to drive away the evil spirit that is believed to be riding on the storm. The Australians kill their storm-demons with boomerangs ; while the Breton peasant, when a wisp of hay is lifted by the wind, throws a knife or fork at the wizard that is supposed to be disporting himself there.

Other powers of nature are similarly treated by the savage, and the custom is continued by his

* J. G. Frazer, *Golden Bough.*

civilised brother without any clear conception of the significance of his own actions. It is unnecessary to discuss the details of locust cursing and the banning of frosts, but the methods of making and preventing rain occupy such a large place in savage life that a detailed account is necessary if we are to understand man's early habits of thought, and how primitive usages developed into elaborate systems of ritual and religion.

The approved methods of rain-making vary considerably according to the fancies of the professors of the art. In Russia, men used to climb lofty trees with a vessel full of water. While seated on their airy perch, two firebrands were struck together to imitate lightning, and a drum beat as a substitute for thunder, during which the rain-maker sprinkled water from his vessel on all sides to produce a miniature shower in sympathy with which rain fell copiously.* This system of producing rain by imitation and sympathy is common in parts of South and South-east Africa, as among Hlubies and Swazies. The rain-doctor goes to a river, from which, with much mystic ceremony, he draws water, which he carries to a cultivated field. He then throws jets from his vessel high into the air, and the falling spray draws down the clouds and causes rain to fall in sympathy. In time of severe drought the Zulus look out for a "heaven bird," which is ordinarily sacred, kill it, and throw it into a pool of water. Then the skies melt in pity for the bird and rain down tears of sorrow upon the earth.† The

* W. Mannhardt. † Bishop Callaway.

Lubare of the Wagogo is lord of heaven and of earth, and gives or withholds rain according as men conduct themselves towards it. New Caledonians dig up a body recently buried, and after they have removed and cleaned the bones they rejoint them and place the skeleton over taro leaves ; water is then poured over it, which the spirit of the man who owned the skeleton takes up and showers down in plenteous rain.* The same motive comes out clearly in the mode of making rain common among peoples of South-eastern Europe. " In times of drought, the Servians strip a girl, clothe her in grass, herbs, and flowers, even her face being hidden with them. Thus disguised, she is called the Dodola, and goes through the village with a troop of girls. They stop before every house ; the Dodola dances, while the other girls form a ring round her singing one of the Dodola songs, and the housewife pours a pail of water over her." † Similar customs are observed by Greeks, Bulgarians and others.

These illustrations, which might be multiplied to any extent, show us clearly that the savage does not place any limitations to his own power over nature, and that early customs, once firmly rooted in the tribal or national mind, are observed by civilised men long after the faith that gave them birth has been forgotten and replaced by systems which, in the interval, may have been changed or modified many times—customs which one moment's reflection shows to be as absurd as they are childish. But absurd as such actions may appear to us, there is

* Turner, *Samoa*.   † J. G. Frazer.

behind them a philosophy, and from them we learn
the processes of the human mind, as, groping after
knowledge, it proceeded on the road to the discovery
of all the facts which make up the sum of the world's
acquirements. Though at first sight the action of
the savage seems as if based on the assumption that
nature is a series of caprices, a closer study con-
vinces us that his reasoning is based on the con-
stancy of nature, or, as we would say, the persistency
of natural laws. The savage expects the same
causes to produce the same results at all times, however inadequate the cause may actually be, and the
universality of this belief proves that it is no mere
local philosophy, which is false root and branch, but
a universal craving after knowledge on the basis of
a philosophy where the premisses are false, but
where, this defect apart, the conclusion is based on
sound reasoning. What we call natural law the
savage ascribes to his own power over the forces of
the physical world.

The reason of this boundless confidence in himself
on the part of primitive man is, that at first supernatural agents are not regarded as greatly superior
to himself, and that at any time he may become
one. These supernatural agents dwell in man, and
their presence make him divine. To him acts of
homage are paid. As the system develops, sacrifices
are offered to him, and he is worshipped as a god.
The office he holds is, or tends to become, hereditary;
in any case, it is elective, and persons holding it are
always sacred, frequently divine. Thus, the nominal
King of the Monbutto is divine, a veritable man-god.

He may not be seen to eat by any one. What he leaves is thrown into a pit set apart for the purpose. Whatever he handles is sacred and may not again be used for any purpose. A guest of even the highest rank and honour may not light his pipe with an ember from the fire that burns before him. To do so would be punished by instant death.* What the results of shaking hands with his majesty would be it is hard to conjecture; probably a tremor reaching to the outermost circle of the universe.

When the Purra, or high priest of the Bulloms, West Africa, goes to a place, all women must, on pain of instant death, keep indoors or hide in the depth of the jungle;† they must keep up a continual clapping of hands while he is pleased to remain, and should any of them be known to have a peep at the Purra, even through a chink, she would be executed instanter for her presumption in gazing on divinity. Jaggas, like many other East African peoples, regard their king as divine,‡ and all his people do him reverence. Before a visitor can be admitted to his presence, he must be sprinkled with medicine by the magician. On all occasions his person is guarded with the most jealous care, and whatever touches him or comes from his person is sacred and must be treated with the utmost reverence;§ as something differing from what was the king's simply, rather as having in itself the elements of divinity from its having belonged to one who is himself a man-god.

Engai—that is, the rain-cloud—placed the father of

* Schweinfurth.　　† Winterbotham.
‡ Krapf.　　§ *Ibid.*

the Wakuafi on the snow mountain, Killimanjaro.
This first ancestor was an incarnation of Engai himself, and was exalted above all men. His children
were demi-gods and the ancestors of the present
ruling chiefs.* From him, or his incarnations,
radiates everything, even the bodies of his subjects,
for he is their god. This same form of king adoration
and homage exists in Shoa, Abyssinia. The Wadoe
address their king as " Lion of Heaven."† When
his majesty coughs or sneezes, all within hearing
say " Muisa," which means, Lion or Lord of Heaven.
The Gingane, or high priest of certain Congo tribes,
is divine.‡ His person is sacred, and he is always
accompanied by a novice who, in the event of his
death, will receive or catch the divine element or
soul which belongs to him in virtue of his office,
and which, but for the novice's presence, might be
lost or stolen.

Among the Baralongs all property belongs to the
chief, as do also the bodies of his subjects. He acts
as his own chief priest ; is invariably called father,
often lord. Zulus and Galekas acknowledge the
chief as universal owner, and regard themselves as
his, body and soul. The Kings of Dahomey and
Ashantee are veritable gods, without any gilding to
conceal their glory ; as is also the Grand Lama of
Thibet. Men pronounce the King of Dahomey's
name with bated breath, fearing the very walls may
whisper of the great name being used profanely.§
Among South African tribes there is a marked aversion to pronouncing the chief's name, and it is never

* Krapf.   † *Ibid.*   ‡ Tucker.   § Rowley.

done when it can by any possibility be avoided by them.

Makusa, the spirit *par excellence* of the Wagogo and Waganda, leaves his quarters in Lake Nyanza at intervals, and takes up his abode in a man or woman, who becomes Lubare,* or, in other words, a god. The Lubare is supreme, not only in matters of faith and sacrifice, but in questions of war and state policy. When councillors were questioned by Mackay regarding the nature of the Lubare, or Makusa who dwelt in the Lubare, they replied that the Lubare is a bull—this because the Lubare represents the principle of universal life. Again, the Lubare was described as a wandering spirit, and finally, as a man who becomes a Lubare. The first is probably the more general belief regarding the Lubare as possessed by Makusa.

When Makusa enters a man he becomes a Lubare, and is removed, by Makusa presumably, about a mile and a half from the margin of the lake, and there waits the advent of the new moon before beginning operations. When the first faint crescent is discerned the king and all his subjects are from that hour under the orders of the Lubare. The king orders a flotilla of canoes to start on a trading expedition; the Lubare hears of it; countermands the king's instructions, and is obeyed. Whatever the divine man orders must be done. If he takes a fancy for a trifle of five hundred heads as a sacrifice, the king's executioners must post themselves on the highways to catch wayfarers till the

* Mackay of Uganda.

requisite number is made up. Or should his fancy
suggest the extermination of a weak neighbouring
tribe, the warriors must be called by beat of drum,
and be on the war-path before the dawn of day.
The king, absolute, despotic, tyrannical as he is,
becomes for the time being the agent through whom
the executive is carried on by the Lubare.

The chief Lakonga, at the south end of the lake,
calls himself a god, and is treated as such by his
people * who prostrate themselves before him as
they approach, and perform such acts of worship as
are rendered to true divinity. At times, however,
there are rival claimants as being descended from
the same god ancestor long before, which is a little
confusing, and has tended to bring the office into
disrepute. Still, the fact remains that the present
ruler claims divinity, and his claim is acknowledged,
though odd sceptics may exist, especially among
those who supported the claims of rivals.

In Laongo the king is worshipped as a god, and
is called Sambee and Pango, words which mean
god.† When rain falls and crops are plentiful they
load him with gifts and honours. If the seasons are
bad, so that crops fail and fish cannot be caught, he
is accused of having a bad heart and is deposed ; but
this belongs rather to the practice of killing the god,
which falls to be discussed in another connection.
Traces of the same kingly divinity can still be found
lingering among the Celtic races of Europe. The
extraordinary sanctity of the chief's person among
Scottish Highlanders of a past generation seems to

* Mackay of Uganda. † J. G. Frazer.

have been nothing else than a lingering survival of divinity in the head of the clan.

From this rapid and fragmentary survey of the position occupied in the world's earliest religious ordinances by the king or ruler, we may safely infer that the claims put forward to divine and supernatural powers by great monarchs like those of ancient Egypt, Mexico, Peru, Japan, and Chaldea, as in the time of Daniel, was not so much the pride of power and the vanity of men accustomed to fulsome flattery and adulation, as a survival of a belief once universal among men. The union of sacred functions and claims to divinity with civil and political power meets us at every turn. It goes to confirm the traditional account given of the sacrificial king at Rome and the origin of the priestly kings in republican Greece, nor does the multiplicity of gods in classical times present the same difficulties which might at first sight be supposed, for among primitive men we find kings who are regarded as divine presiding over particular departments of nature ; departmental kings, as Mr. Frazer calls them.* At the mouth of the Congo resides Namvula Ruma as "king of the rain and storm." His functions do not extend beyond his own department, but there he reigns supreme, and is regarded as divine by mariners and agriculturists. In Abyssinia an office exists known as "the priesthood of the Alfai," which is hereditary and kingly. He, too, is a king of rain, and is supposed to avert drought and produce necessary showers. Should he in this

---

* J. G. Frazer, *Golden Bough.*

disappoint the people's expectations, he is stoned to death, and a successor chosen ; no easy task when the heavens are as brass and the ground as iron. The offices performed by the mysterious kings of fire and water in the backwoods of Cambodia, seem to have a close resemblance to those of the king of rain and storm at the Congo and the priest of the Alfai in Abyssinia. Of the mysterious Cambodian monarchs not much is known, and their existence might have passed as a myth, but for the real king exchanging presents with them annually. No one travelled to their domains, and the gifts were passed on from tribe to tribe till they reached their destination, after which the return present of a wax candle and two calabashes began an erratic pilgrimage to the king who had despatched the gifts to his mysterious subjects and equals, or more than equals. The functions of the kings of fire and water were purely spiritual. They claimed no civil power or political authority, and lived simply as peasants. They lived apart, and gifts were brought furtively and left where they could find them. Their offices are hereditary and last seven years, but owing to the hard and solitary life many are said to die during their term of office. Naturally the dignity is not coveted, and like the Alfai priesthood there is difficulty in finding suitable candidates from among those who are eligible for office.

Did the scope of our inquiry permit, a king of the wood and of the sea could be found among primitive men, but enough has been said to show the general relations subsisting between man, as he first began to look out on the world and wander hither and thither over the face of the globe, and the supernatural, which to him was an utterly unknown world. We shall now turn to the consideration of the care man bestowed on those who, according to his conception of the constitution of the universe, were its supernatural agents or divinities.

CHAPTER II

WE have seen in the preceding chapter that the king or divine ruler was endowed with supernatural powers, by means of which he was able to regulate rain and sunshine, the growth of crops and the capture of bird, beast, and fish. His power over nature was analogous to that which he exercised over his subjects. He had but to will in order to have his purpose accomplished, neither nature nor subject having a choice in the matter. But with strange contradiction of thought, while the course of nature was dependent upon and subject to the king's will, phenomena were often supposed to be not only independent of him, but inimical to his interests and dangerous to his life, as were also certain objects, should he touch or even see them. His will was supreme in regard to all conditions of wind and weather, sunshine and shadow; but his body occupied the anomalous position of at once influencing the forces of nature and being liable to take harm from the simplest elements. His divine organism was so finely balanced that a movement of head or hand might disturb the equilibrium of the universe, and if in an evil moment he gave hidden forces a wrong impulse, it might entail such wholesale destruction as the falling of the sky or the hurling the world away into limitless space. Even such a simple act as drinking a glass of wine in the presence of another was so fraught with danger that the spectator had to be put to death. One case is on record in which the king's son, a boy of twelve, saw his father drink accidentally. He was seized, finely arrayed, and killed. After that his body was quartered and sent about with a proclamation that he had seen the king drink.* No more was needed.

Of this class of divine rulers is the Mikado of Japan, a descendant of Izangi, who gave birth to the god of fire. After her death, her spouse, who was her own brother, purified himself by bathing in a stream of running water. As he threw his garments on the bank—the gods seem to have been familiar with the modern tailor's art in those days —fresh deities were born from each article. From his left eye emerged the goddess of the Sun, who was the ancestress of all the divine generations of rulers.† The following account of the Mikado was written about two hundred years ago : ‡

" Even to this day princes descended of this family, more particularly those who sit on the throne, are looked upon as persons most holy in themselves, and as popes by birth. And in order to preserve those advantageous notions in the minds of their subjects they are obliged to take uncommon care of their sacred persons, and to do such

* J. G. Frazer, *Golden Bough*.   † Chamberlain, *Things Japanese*.
‡ Kaempfer, "History of Japan," in Pinkerton's *Voyages and Travels*.

things which, examined according to the customs
of other nations, would be thought ridiculous and
impertinent. He thinks that it would be very pre-
judicial to his dignity and holiness to touch the
ground with his feet; for this reason, when he
intends to go anywhere he must be carried thither
on men's shoulders. Much less will they suffer
that he should expose his sacred person to the open
air, and the sun is not thought worthy to shine on
his head. There is such a holiness ascribed to
all the parts of his body that he dares to cut off
neither his hair, nor his beard, nor his nails. However, lest he should grow too dirty, they may clean
him in the night when he is asleep, because, they
say, that which is taken from his body at that
time hath been stolen from him, and that such a
theft does not prejudice his holiness or his dignity.

In ancient times he was obliged to sit on the
throne for some hours every morning with the imperial crown on his head, but to sit altogether like a
statue, without stirring either hands or feet, nor,
indeed, any part of his body, because by this
means it was thought that he could preserve peace
and tranquillity in his empire, for if, unfortunately,
he turned himself on one side or other, or if he
looked a good while towards any part of his
dominions, it was apprehended that war, famine,
fire, or some great misfortune was near at hand to
desolate the country. But it having been afterwards discovered that the imperial crown was the
palladium which by its mobility could preserve peace
in the empire, it was thought expedient to deliver

his imperial person, consecrated only to idleness and pleasures, from this burthensome duty, and therefore the crown is at present placed on the throne for some hours every morning. His victuals must be dressed every time in new pots, and served at table in new dishes, both very clean and neat, but made only of common clay, that without any considerable expense they may be laid aside, or broken, after they have served once. They are generally broken for fear they should come into the hands of laymen ; for they believe religiously that if a layman should presume to eat his food out of these sacred dishes, it would swell, and inflame his mouth and throat." So much for the Mikado's habits of life.

But this guarding of kings is not confined to an advanced cult. Among primitive peoples we find priestly persons and divine kings guarded with equal jealousy and care. At Shark Point, West Africa, the king lives alone in a wood. He may never leave his house. He may not touch a woman. On no account must he quit his royal chair, even to sleep, for in that case the wind would die down and all navigation would be stopped.* The supreme ruler at Congo is such another. Regarded as a god on earth, no subject would, on any consideration, taste the new crop till an offering of it is made to him. When he leaves his residence to visit other parts of his territory, all married persons are under obligation to observe stringent laws of continence, any violation of which would prove immediately fatal to Chitome.

* J. G. Frazer, *Golden Bough.*

Were he to die a natural death, the world would be
annihilated.*

Illustrations might be multiplied, but whether in
Africa, Japan, or the South Sea Islands, the order
and regularity of nature is bound up with the life of
the ruler. It is evident he must be regarded by his
people as at once a source of untold blessing and
inexpressible danger to society. The care of his
person must be their first consideration in their
home and foreign policy, for any accident, through
oversight or lack of vigilance, might prove fatal to
the State. If he gives them rain, sunshine, genial
warmth, successful hunting and fishing,.he can also
withhold these blessings and reverse the order of
nature. When the working of visible phenomena
is so closely bound up with his person that hurting his
toe might set up such a tremor as would overthrow
the foundations of the earth, the care bestowed on
his safe keeping must be infinite. For their own
safety his subjects must surround him with restrictions and safeguards. There must be set and accurate rules for the regulation of his conduct both
public and private. So it happens that his life is
valuable only in so far as he discharges the functions
for which he exists.

When he fails to order the course of nature so as
to benefit his people, his deposition is not only a
duty but a necessity. The homage and worship he
received is turned into contempt and hatred, for he
is not only useless, he is now positively hurtful.
Disgraced as a ruler, he is disgraced as a god, and

* J. G. Frazer, quoting Labat.

then put to an ignominious death. During his life,
or at least his reign, he lives hedged in by such
restrictions and limitations that he ceases to be
a free agent, even when his people prostrate
themselves before him, and offer to him the most
costly gifts and sacrifices, perhaps their sons or
daughters.

Of the divine King of Loango it is said that the
greater his divinity the more restrictions or taboos
he must observe. These regulate all his actions, his
walking and his sitting, his eating and drinking, his
sleeping and waking.* To the same restrictions the
heir is subjected from infancy, only that the number
of observances during childhood are comparatively
few, but increasing in number, till on his reaching
manhood he is lost in the swaddling-clothes of taboos.
The kings of ancient Egypt were, and in fact all rulers
now worshipped as divine are, subject to the same life
of immobility and inaction. King Egbo, West Africa,
when he went abroad was concealed in an ark as
became a divine and supernatural being. This was
carried on the shoulders of men who were set apart
for the sacred office, and were themselves sacred
persons.† The sacred bearers still remain, but when
Egbo, who has left the palace to the actual ruler,
and now lives in a sacred grove that none may
enter or explore, goes abroad, the ark contains
but a dummy which is followed by the reigning
monarch walking on foot. The king prefers the
advantages of substantial power to the honours of
divinity, and so does homage to the ghost of his

* Bastian. † Waddell.

own divinity, rather than enter the sacred box himself, to be the toy of party politicians.

When the office of ruler grew to be at once so burdensome and so useless there could be but one result. Men of action closed up the god in a box and went on foot. Contenting themselves with the substance of power, they left the honour and semblance to some nerveless aspirant to the priesthood who was satisfied with homage and honour in his sacred retreat, while his rival ruled the kingdom. This in course of time would lead to a separation between the offices of ruler and high priest, and so we gradually reach a farther stage in the development of human thought and the evolution of deity as that presented itself to primitive man. So burdensome did the office of king become, in the days when kings were divine, that we find in West Africa, when a king dies, a family council secretly held to elect his successor. The hapless victim is seized, bound hand and foot, and then thrown into the fetish-house till he consents to accept the kingly honours thus forced upon him. The Gallas of the East elect their king once in eight years. They are selected from five families who are royal, and through whom the succession to the throne is carefully kept up. They have a custom called Rab which compels the four families out of office to destroy all their children; those reigning for the time being allowed to rear theirs.* It is doubtless from such examples being common, that facts such as those recorded in the Book of Exodus regarding

* Krapf.

the drowning of infants became possible as a political precaution. Powerful kings like those of ancient Egypt, or of Dahomey and Ashantee in modern times, may succeed in combining a vigorous policy with sacred functions and the idea of a man-god, but the tendency is towards degeneration and extinction. When a man ceases to move from his royal chair, to see any of his subjects except those whose interests it is to tell him only what suits their own purpose; when a movement of hand or head is dangerous to the stability of the world, and that he must give all needed blessings while carefully wrapped up in the swaddling-bands of taboo, his final disappearance cannot be long delayed. His memory lasts, but it becomes a shadow merging into ancestor worship, or kept in a closed ark in the fetish-house.

There was another, and perhaps a more powerful, reason among primitive men why those who were men of action should decline the honours of divinity, and that was the practice of killing the god.* Ancient mythology has made us familiar with the idea of the death of the gods, and if divine and spiritual deities were subject to decrepitude, decay, and death, how much more the human gods of primitive man ? It was natural that men in far-away times should bestow the greatest care on their divinities, and surround them with taboos and restrictions calculated to keep them out of harm's way. But no care could make human gods immortal, and the worshippers had to take account

* Frazer, *Golden Bough.*

of the stern fact and meet it as best they might. If the course of nature depended on the god, what might not old age and imbecility bring upon the nation ? Should his powers decay and his perceptions become dimmed, he might in a second precipitate calamities which would prove disastrous to himself and his subjects. The world itself might be thrown out of place, and projected no one knew where, for in those days the powers of divine persons were not restricted to " projecting " bits of flimsy French paper in the form of letters with indifferent spelling.

There was only one way open by which the danger could be met, and that was by putting the god to death while still in the full possession of his faculties or on the first appearance of outward symptoms of decay, as a grey hair or hollow tooth, and thus secure the entrance of his soul or divinity into his successor.* Should he die a natural death, even in his prime, and before the dangers of decay appeared, his soul might be stolen, or stray away into winter and night to wander for ever. If the world were to collapse on the King of Congo dying a natural death, such a contingency could only be averted by dispatching him to the land of shadows by violent means. So it was that when a king fell ill his heir and successor entered his house with a rope and club, and either strangled or clubbed him to death.†
" The King of Quiteva, in Eastern Africa, ranked with deity,"‡ and this continued till one of the kings lost a tooth, and feeling no disposition to

---

* J. G. Frazer, *Golden Bough.*   † Labat.   ‡ Dos Santos.

follow the practice of his predecessors by quitting
the upper air on the appearance of the first bodily
defect, published to his people that he had lost a
front tooth, in order that "when they might behold
they might yet be able to recognise him." The historian continues : "He declared at the same time
that he was resolved on living and reigning as long
as he could, esteeming his existence requisite for the
welfare of his subjects. He at the same time loudly
condemned the practice of his predecessors, whom
he taxed with imprudence, nay, even with madness,
for condemning themselves to death for casual accidents to their persons; and abrogating this mortal
law, he ordained that all his successors, if sane,
should follow the precedent he gave, and the new
law established by him."*

This man, whose name is not given, was as bold a
reformer as was Ergamenes of Meroe. There the
kings were worshipped as gods, but whenever the
priests sent a message that the king must die, he
voluntarily submitted to be put to death. When
the summons came to Ergamenes he replied to it by
putting the priests themselves to the sword, thus
reversing the order, and putting an end to the
practice once for all. In Unyoro the king is killed
by his own wives when seriously ill.

Nor is the custom of killing the divine king confined to Africa. The King of Calicut could only
rule twelve years, after which he must publicly commit suicide according to an approved method ; a
method only a little less suggestive of the shambles

* Dos Santos.

than the Harakiri of the Japanese. The first modification of the Calicut law of succession was made towards the end of the seventeenth century, when at the end of the twelve years a tent was pitched, and the king had a great feast lasting ten or twelve days, at the end of which any one might kill him and gain the crown.* To do so he must cut his way, sword in hand, through the king's bodyguard to reach him in his tent. The desperate attempt was at times made but never with success.

They were bold men who ventured on drastic reforms in far-away days ; bolder still were those who ventured to curb the power of the priests after the offices of ruler and high-priest came to be separated, as not a few European monarchs discovered to their cost when kept standing, barefooted and bareheaded, waiting the pleasure of an arrogant ecclesiastic. But limitations were not put to the power of the priesthood without a long period of transition, during which many expedients were adopted to preserve time-honoured usage, and adjust that to the inevitable, as represented by a truculent ruler who wished to enjoy the upper air as long as nature permitted him to do so, and who acquired awkward habits of answering the arguments of philosophers with sword-cut or gallows. To only one of such expedients can we refer, that of temporary kings or substitutes.

Where kings were put to death at the end of fixed periods or on the appearance of the first signs of

* Hamilton, quoted by J. G. Frazer.

decay, rulers would anxiously endeavour to discover
a means of evading the letter of the law while giving
such obedience to its spirit as would satisfy their
subjects and worshippers. Some boldly set the law
at defiance by refusing to submit to its requirements.
Others sought out substitutes, and introduced to
men's minds the idea of one taking, in a grave
crisis, the place of another, and being regarded as the
person he represented; his own individuality being
lost in the act of self-surrender and substitution.
He became the king, the very man-god whom people
worshipped, in his office and act. The real king in
fact died, and in resuming the government it was a
new king who ascended the throne to reign for
another stated period. At first a relative of the
king would act as substitute, but this could not
continue long without the sense of justice inherent
in man revolting against such a barbarous practice,
and a slave or condemned criminal would be substituted for a brother or son. This substitute,
whether son or slave, was for a time clothed with
kingly authority and lived in regal state, while the
king retired into private life. Even the royal harem
might be invaded by the temporary king, a fact, when
we consider the extraordinary jealousy with which
they were guarded, which shows clearly that only for
the most weighty reasons could such a thing be permitted. It could only be in order that the temporary
king should be invested with full regal authority
without restriction or limitation. At the end of the
time allowed, the temporary king was put to death—
killed as a god—the king resuming office. The

custom is in some places softened down still more, and the substitute is not actually put to death, a mock execution being sufficient. This latter custom is observed in Cambodia, where the temporary king receives the revenues during his three days of office, as is also done by the same functionary in Siam, only the latter seizes ships entering harbour, and holds them till redeemed. At the end of his term of office he goes to a field and draws nine furrows, where seed is sown by old women. When the ninth furrow is finished, the spectators rush to pick up the seed just sown to mix with their own, and so secure a plentiful crop. This temporary king is known as "Lord of the Heavenly Host."* These customs, and especially the killing of the king or his substitute, introduce us to the earliest form of human sacrifice, a system which developed to such gigantic proportions as men's conception of the supernatural advanced from the ideas of human divinities to personal spiritual existences, whether as the spirit of corn or vegetation generally, the powers of nature or the souls of departed ancestors. To the development of this form of religion and worship we shall now turn.

* J. G. Frazer, quoting Pallegoix.

CHAPTER III

EVOLUTION OF DEITY

To form a correct conception of African and other primitive peoples, it is necessary to have some acquaintance with the doctrine of souls, as that is understood by savage men. This throughout Africa is vague, and the results of inquiry are far from satisfactory. One hears accounts of souls, differing in all essentials, from men who observe the same forms of worship and are subject to the same system of government. The facts on which all are agreed are few and easily enumerated. All men have souls, even idiots, though some deny this, and the departure of the soul from the body is death. The soul is air, breath, wind, spirit, or it may be regarded as being all these, or having their essence. It is invisible, but in miniature an exact reproduction of the man. It is his shadow, reflection, what speaks in him. During sleep, or when a man is in a faint, his soul is absent from the body, but returns with restored animation. Should a person in a faint be removed from one place to another, as taking him out of his house into the open air, he could not recover, as the soul would return to the spot where the man fainted, and not finding him there, would go away. Again, a sleeper must not be rudely or hurriedly awakened, lest his soul, like Baal of old, should be on a journey, and have no time to return to re-enter the body. In that case the man might not die, but he would cease to be human, and go to wander for ever in the forest like those corpses raised by the art of witchcraft, and who are doomed to an eternal wandering in mist and rain. The spirit or soul, in the case of temporary absence, leaves the body by the natural openings, especially the nostrils, and must re-enter by the way it went ; hence placing a handkerchief over the face of a sleeper would be highly reprehensible, as it might, probably would, lead to certain death. So would closing the mouth, should the soul have left by that door.

At death the soul leaves the body to return no more. Its leaving is not regarded as voluntary, as death—that is, the expulsion of the soul—is most frequently the work of wizards ; but in any case it cannot re-enter that body "whose eyes shall never see the sun again." Where does the soul go when it leaves the body, either temporarily or permanently ? During the absence of sleep it may "visit the sleeper's friend in a dream," or it may "flit about the roof ; " in either case its return is prompt the moment the slumberer begins to move his limbs. "The soul hears even a long breath, should it be with my friend far away," said a Kaffir once to me in a moment of unwonted confidence. At death the soul hovers near the body till the latter is buried, and then takes up its abode in the great world of spirits, except in those cases in which it enters an animal or object to watch over the doings of men.

But souls are almost as liable to danger from external circumstances as human divinities are. They may be stolen, like a man's purse ; snatched away in a whiff of whirlwind, or lost through carelessness or neglect. Should a South African native see an Incante, his soul would be snatched away and he would die on the spot. When a " river calls," he must enter it, but only to drown in its deep waters. The Hili living there demands his soul. He may be bewitched by wizards, and his soul stolen, leaving him a ghostly wanderer in fen and forest. A Zulu will not look into a dark pool, as there is a creature " behind the reflection " that will steal away his shadow, and he dies. To all mirrors and reflecting surfaces there is the same objection. In either case the soul is snatched away by the devil. So it happens that mirrors being " expressly invented by the devil for his purposes," people in civilised countries cover up theirs whenever there is a death in the house. To this day, in the Highlands of Scotland, all mirrors are carefully covered over with white cloths the moment a person expires. The same is done in Madagascar ; the custom is not extinct in England.

Such beliefs regarding the nature and habits of souls linger in odd corners of Europe in a much more distinct form than the custom of covering mirrors. In Greece, when a new house is being built, they have a peculiar method of giving stability to the building. For this purpose a cock is killed and its blood allowed to flow on the foundation-stone. Another and a more effectual method is for the builder to entice a man, on some pretext, to enter where the builders are at work and then measure his shadow by stealth. This measure placed under the foundation-stone, gives the house absolute stability. The person whose shadow was measured " dies within a year," but that is a secondary matter with the contractor.* This is beyond doubt a survival of an ancient custom, and a belief that a man's soul and his shadow were identical, or in any case indissolubly bound to one another. I remember hearing my father tell of an old Highland tradition that those who practised the black art cast no shadow. They had sold their souls to the devil for supernatural power, and their immortal part being his by right and possession, the body cast no shadow from the sun, soul and shadow being one. Another danger of the soul was slow expulsion by sorcery, but this belongs rather to the subject of witchcraft, under which it falls to be considered.

Having thus seen the nature of the soul and a few of its dangers as these are conceived by savage men, we can the more easily proceed to the study of spiritual divinities as distinguished from, or evolved out of, incarnate gods. We shall begin with South Africa. There every man worships the spirits of his departed ancestors, especially those recently deceased. In Africa, as elsewhere, old ghosts are not of much account. The father's spirit must

* J. G. Frazer, *Golden Bough*.

be worshipped and his wants supplied by sacrifice; the grandfather's must be honoured and his known wishes regarded, but the poor old great-grandfather may sit in his horn in the corner and no one pay any special regard to him, unless, indeed, he happened to be a noted man, as the founder of a family or sept. The clans worship in the same manner the spirits of their departed chiefs, and where all the clans composing a tribe are supposed to be descended from a common ancestor, the spirits of departed tribal chiefs are a kind of supreme, or at least superior, deities. When a tribe is composed of different clans this powerful element of union, the worship of a common ancestor, is wanting, as each clan looks to its hereditary chief as its true divinity. They have no very definite idea of the mode of existence of their deities, only they inhabit the old places and are always at hand. A man cannot perform an action unknown to the gods, though thieves disguise themselves to deceive divinity. This, however, is never effectual, as the wise men will say, "A thief is always known, though we cannot say his name."

Closely connected with the doctrine of divinity is that of other spirits than the souls of ancestors. Those most commonly met with are water or river spirits, inhabiting deep pools where there are strong eddies and under-currents. These are wicked and malevolent beings, and are never credited with any good. Whatever they possess they keep, and seize on anything which comes within their reach, especially the souls of men. Other spirits reside in forests, mountains and rocky caverns. They

frequently leave their haunts and assume animal
form, as baboon, wolf, wild dog, snake, or lizard. This
is always for pure mischief, and their malevolent
designs can only be averted by the use of charms
prepared by a magician, and sacrifice. Moremo, the
god of the Bechuanas, was malicious and cunning.*
They never hesitated to express their indignation
when he disappointed them, by bitter invective and
cursing. This same method was suggested to Job
by his wife : " Curse God and die," said that virago.
When they had good crops, Moremo got all the
credit of it, and was patronised as a generous, good-
natured kind of a god after all. Evidently, from
the accounts that have reached us, Bechuana religion is not very profound, nor is their god very
consistent.

As we move northwards we find the deities under-
going considerable modification, and along the west
coast we make the acquaintance of Fetish and
Fetish idols, hardly a trace of which is to be found
in east and east-central Africa. These totems or
sacred animals become the clan badges, and from
the animals held sacred we can recognise scattered
remnants of tribes separated by hundreds of miles,
and having hardly any customs in common except
the sacred animal as their clan badge. Throughout
the whole continent we meet with customs, ritual,
ceremonial acts, and other observances which have
at first sight no appearance of being connected with
any religious belief, but which have a religious
significance. And this is consistent with savage

* Livingstone.

thought, which always connects the most insignifi-
cant action that is unusual with what is supernatural,
as a cock crowing in the evening* or a crane alighting
on a house-top.   Actions done by individuals may
influence the whole policy of a tribe for generations
either for good or evil.   For example, the natives of
Senjero, Abyssinia, sell only female slaves, never
men or boys, and any one selling a male would
bring upon himself the wrath of the gods, even if
he could hope to escape a visit from the executioner.
The origin of the custom is said to have been that a
king long ago, when kings were divine, had ordered a
man to kill his wife and bring him a piece of her flesh
for the cure of an ailment from which he suffered.
The man refused to comply with the king's order,
and saved his wife alive.   She was next sent for and
told what had happened, after which she was asked
to slay her husband and bring a piece of his flesh to
the king.   This the ungrateful woman did, and
ever since then a Senjero man may sell his daughter,
or even his wife, but a man never.†   Human sacrifices to their divinities are common among the people
of Senjero.   This, so runs the legend, was introduced
long ago, when the seasons got confused, summer and
winter being so mixed up that no crops ripened.
The priests " ordered many families to sacrifice their
first-born," and the rulers of the town to raze a huge
iron pillar which stood outside the gate.   The base

* A lady living in the highlands of Scotland a few years ago had a cock
that crowed in the evening.   Her peasant neighbours urged her to kill it.
She consulted a local gentleman, who replied to her question : " No, no,
Mrs. Brown, there is no harm in the creature, none whatever : but I will
tell you what, if I were in your place I would wring that cock's neck."

† Krapf.

of the pillar, like "the stump of the roots" of the tree in Nebuchadnezzar's vision, was to be left, and it and the throne to be sprinkled with the blood of the victims. After this was done the seasons resumed their normal course; * but in memory of the event, and to prevent its recurrence, the sacrifices are observed annually, and both throne and the spot where the pillar stood sprinkled with blood. This myth, the iron pillar apart, is probably a transcript of what the historian witnessed with his own eyes. These obscure practices and legends point back to a time when the spirit of vegetation, or creative energy, was worshipped and sacrifices offered to it. The confusion of the seasons and their readjustment by sacrifice has undoubtedly a close connection with the worship of the spirit of growth. Another curious custom in Senjero is the throwing of a slave into Lake Umo by dealers in men when setting out on a raiding expedition.† The sacrifice is to the deity of the lake, in order that he may, from the victim given as a seed-corn, give a plentiful crop.

Among the Gallas the priests occupy a position distinct from the magicians or exorcists. They have the highest place in all religious ceremonies, and receive special honour and homage from their votaries. Here we find trees and vegetation occupying a prominent place in all religious observances and acts of worship. So marked is this characteristic that it is more akin to the worship and sacrifice of the Khonds of India than what we are familiar with in most parts of Africa. The

---

* Krapf.   † *Ibid.*

Galla priest will sacrifice only under the woda-tree. In it, spirit, "even a higher spirit," dwells, and no man dare fell a woda-tree. If he does so, he forfeits his life.* The tree itself is sacred, and so too is the woda-mabi, or groves where it grows by the River Hawash where the great yearly festivals are held. At these gatherings the tree spirit is worshipped by offerings and sacrifice.† Nor is the worship of tree spirits peculiar to the Gallas. We meet with it in Lithuania, in Bavaria, and in Southern Europe. The Ovaons of Bengal have a festival in spring, while the sál-trees are in blossom, because they think that at that time the marriage of earth is celebrated, and sál-flowers are necessary for the ceremony. On the day appointed, the villagers, accompanied by their priest, gather the flowers in a forest where a goddess is supposed to dwell. Next day the priest visits each house carrying the flowers with him. The women as he approaches bring out water to wash his feet and do him obeisance. Then he dances with them, placing flowers in their hair, after which they drench him with water.‡ This ceremony is supposed to have an influence upon the course of the weather, especially the rainfall, and the spirit of the sacred sál-tree is represented by both the flowers and the priest who brings them, introducing us to the double representation of the spirit of vegetation, by a person and object, as that survives in the Grass king of Sommerberg or the May Bride of Altmark.§

* Krapf.　　　　　　　† *Ibid.*
‡ Dalton.　　　　　　§ Monnier.

The Gallas have no idols, but revere objects and
animals, serpents being specially sacred. One variety
of snake they regard as having been the mother of
the human family. This same belief was a prominent
feature of the ancient paganism of Abyssinia. The
supreme Galla deity is water; under him, or her, are
two subordinate gods, a masculine, Oglie, to whom
cows are sacrificed in June and July, and his consort
Atetie, whose offerings are made in September, and
may consist of animals or fruits. She is the goddess
of fecundity, and women are her principal votaries;
but as she can also make the earth " prolific," offerings are made to her for that purpose.* These
divinities represent the creative and fructifying
powers of nature, and this nature-worship meets us
under different forms in all parts of the Continent.
Even the Gold Coast moon-dance is an act of homage
done to the mother of all.

Passing from the Gallas to the Waganga, the
same essentials are met with in the national worship.
There a cocoa-nut is hung up at the village gate
while the crops are ripening. This, curiously enough,
is to prevent theft, as any one touching the fruits of
the earth while it is there would be visited with the
vengeance of the earth goddess. A secondary object
served is the protection of the crops from injury.
An empty cocoa-nut shell is placed on graves, and
filled now and then with tembo, for without this the
spirit could not exist. Tembo to them represents
the spirit or essence of the earth's fruits: the
life-blood of nature.

* Krapf.

Of this earth divinity the visible representative is the Muansa. This is simply a log of wood, hollowed out in a particular manner, so that when rubbed it emits sounds resembling the roaring and bellowing of wild animals.* It is carried about in solemn procession at all great festivals, for in it the god resides. If at such times it were seen by women or children they would fall down dead. Should a woman, after seeing the Muansa, survive, she would become barren. So, when the god roars, women must hide in the woods till it is carried back to its house. Besides the great festivals, as that of first-fruits, the god roars when the tribe sacrifices for rain, or when men go to the forest to strangle a deformed infant, which is invariably done, as is the case also with a cross-birth or abnormal presentation. The Muansa is the centre of the religious life of the tribe, and is a survival akin to the Egbo of the West Coast. The observances connected with it leave no doubt as to the intention of the institution, that is, the deification of nature, especially corn and vegetation generally. To cut a cocoa-nut tree is equivalent to matricide : " The mother nourishes her infant ; the cocoa-nut tree men. Does an infant destroy its mother? Should a man kill the spirit of the tree that is the bread of the people? " Other Waganga and Waneka religious observances will fall to be considered under oaths and ordeals.

These illustrations of the religious beliefs of East and Central Africa are sufficient for our present purpose, but before passing to the discussion of the

* Krapf.

divinities of the West Coast we may glance at one
phase of a class of social customs extending from
the Cape of Good Hope to the banks of the Nile,
and which are substantially the same among all
peoples over that vast area, though with infinite
variety of detail in the manner of their performance. I refer to the ceremonies and usages connected with the initiation of young people into
manhood and womanhood at the age of puberty.
In South Africa circumcision and intonjane are
universal. The details of these ceremonies vary,
but the object is the same in all. The usual ritual
connected with circumcision is as follows : At the
season of the year when crops are beginning to
ripen, all the young men of a locality are circum-
cised by the village doctor, and are then insolated in
huts, previously prepared, at some distance from
the ordinary dwellings, generally near the edge of a
clump of trees. Men are appointed to watch over
the neophytes, and to prevent their having inter-
course of any kind whatsoever with women. They
daub the young men all over with a pure white
clay, which for the period of probation is their dis-
tinguishing badge. During their novitiate they are
subjected to considerable privations. What butcher's
meat they receive they must steal, and as every
one is on the alert when "white boys" are about,
stealing is by no means a simple art, nor is failure
in the attempt the end of the affair. For failure
they are unmercifully beaten by their tutors, while
a successful foray is worthy of all praise. They are
compelled to do violent bodily exercise in dancing

and running, and are often kept awake for several consecutive nights. They are beaten with saplings and deprived of food, all of which is meant to render them hardy and indifferent to pain, and also as a privation before they receive that full license which is an essential portion of their initiation. At the close of these preliminary ceremonies the white clay is washed off their bodies ; they receive new garments, and then repair to the residence of the chief, where the elders of the tribe and a great concourse of men and women have already assembled. Their bodies are now anointed with oil. Harangues by the minister of war, magician, and bards follow as to their duties to their chief in peace and war. Arms are put into their hands, and they thereby receive the privilege of manhood. A great festival follows, continued for several days and nights. The customs sanctioned by law and usage at these festivals are generally described as obscene. They are certainly such as to lead to the inference that the whole ceremony of initiation is based on the principle of doing homage to the powers of nature.

In the lake region of Central Africa, and especially among the Wayao, the "mysteries" are performed at a corresponding period of life, and there, even more than in the South, it is evident the object is to honour the budding powers of nature as a divinity. The corresponding ceremonies through which young women pass do not admit of description in a popular work ; the object is clearly the same.

When we ask a native to explain the purpose of

these ceremonial usages, he replies that without
them the young folk would always remain children,
and never could become men and women in the
proper sense. There seems to be no distinct philosophy to explain the custom : " it was always so,
and if our people neglected it we would die ;" which
means, gradually decay and disappear as a people.
Only when the details are carefully studied—the
ill-usage and privation of the preliminary stage,
the unchecked license of the festival, and manhood
not being attained without both—and compared
with other customs common everywhere, do we
come to understand that the object is to do homage
to nature; that the beatings and fastings may even
be symbolical of putting the person, or at least the
spirit of creative and reproductive energy, to death,
to be revived, honoured, almost worshipped, during
the festival which closes the ceremonies.

These ceremonies are performed while the crops
are still green but approaching maturity, by sacred
persons whose office is religious. Among some
tribes, as the Hottentots, circumcision must not be
performed with a knife, but with a sharp bit of
quartz. Blood must be encouraged to flow to a
certain extent. The festival marking the close of
the ceremonies must be held before harvest operations are officially commenced, and on the part of
the performers there must be a display of the
utmost vital energy in dancing, wrestling, and
other exercises. The homage due to the goddess
presiding over, or residing in, such powers is the
true significance of the customs and ritual belonging

to the period when youth emerges into manhood
and womanhood.   Nor does this view lack confirmation from the usages of other countries and times.
Harvest festivals are, and have been, akin to the
worship of Bacchus, with the rites of Venus added.
Men and women who are modest, well-behaved, and
in all respects reputable members of society, abandon
themselves at the season of first-fruits to the gods
and goddesses of nature till satiety and disgust
recall them to their senses again.   Such revels are
not the exclusive privilege of savages, for the conduct of the Israelites regarding the Midianites
whom they conquered is a case in point.   So, too,
under other and far different conditions, the worship of the Corinthian Venus and the practice
common in Indian temples show the same honours
and homage, even worship given to the powers of
nature.   And this is nothing else than the worship
of the spirit of creative or reproductive energy in
the animal world, as we have already seen in
connection with the growth of trees, corn, and
vegetation generally.   The deity is Mother Earth ;
the worship, to ensure her good offices in continuing
her bounteous office of reproduction.

The West Coast of Africa is the land of fetish.
How this system originated it is impossible to determine, but there are indications which seem to point
back to its beginnings as a separate religious system.
Among many African tribes it is common to preserve bones, and especially skulls, of ancestors as
relics of the dead.*   These were supposed to be the

* Rowley, *Africa Unveiled.*

abode, temporary or permanent, of the departed soul, and were tended and guarded with all the reverence due to an ancestral spirit itself. From reverence and filial piety the transition to worship would be natural and easy. The soul dwelling in the skull was able to give or withhold certain blessings, and when treated with the respect due to it, could be of great service to the devout descendants who kept and tended it. In this way may have originated at once the worship of fetish, and the well-known African habit of giving the aged a help to leave the world, on the assumption that their bones and disembodied spirits would be of greater service to the living than their bodily presence, when age and infirmity had rendered them helpless. The attention bestowed on an invisible spirit residing in a well-cleaned skull, would not be more troublesome than that required by an aged grandfather, while the former in activity and power to benefit his descendants was vastly superior. At first each family would preserve and tend its own relics, but with the lapse of time their care would devolve on the priests, and with the accumulation of bones suitable receptacles would be provided, developing gradually into special houses or temples consecrated for this purpose, and sacred. From such relic-reverence and worship to fetish would be such an easy transition that no revolution in religious thought would be needed to accomplish it, and once the departed spirit could take up its abode in another object than a bone of its original owner, the growth of fetish objects would proceed apace. The magician, by the exercise of his own supernatural power, could impart to any object a sacred character and make it the home of the soul. For a similar reason he could impart to objects, as necklets, virtues for the protection of the wearer, this object being but a lower form of fetish through which the supernatural influence for protection came to be imparted to the possessor; only, in this case its virtues were restricted to the person on whom the magician bestowed it. Where relic-worship became common the object charmed by the magician would naturally be supposed to be the home of a guardian spirit, and if rudely carved into the image of a man the connection between it and a departed ancestor needed no demonstration. Once this principle became established there would be no limit to the multiplication of fetishes. And so it is that any object in nature may be the abode of spirits. An islet in a lake, a sharp pinnacle of rock, a stone above water in a river, a human bone, a carved image, a ram's horn, or even a man's weapons, may be fetish and have spirits dwelling in them. Fetish brings victory in war, success in fishing, hunting, or trading. It cures all ailments from insanity to sterility.* It preserves life or destroys it, according to the intention of the votary and the nature of the offering.† Its uses are as wide as are the necessities of man, and it can be adapted to every circumstance of life.

But this is not much worse than certain customs still lingering in obscure corners of England.

---

* Rowley.   † Winterbotham.

One of these, known as "Toad-day," seems to carry us back to the days of the Druids, or even an earlier and pre-Aryan period. On Toad-day people resort to a "wise man," or in other words a wizard, to purchase a charm or fetish which is to protect them and theirs from injury for a year. This charm consists of a leg torn from a living toad, which the purchaser devoutly wears about his person.* In Scotland "wise women" cure rheumatism by giving the patient a potato which he must carry in his trousers pocket. While it is in his possession, and carried according to prescription, he is exempt from attack. I once heard a shrewd, long-headed farmer say : "I ha'e haen a twinge o' rheumatics. I had a tatie I got frae a wife, but I slipped it oot o' my pouch amang a wheen twine." The potato being lost or mislaid, his old enemy had returned.

We have seen how religion, when the king ceases to be worshipped as a man-god, tends to pass over to a deification of the powers of nature, associating with these the reproductive energy of departed priests or ancestors. These, or their spirit, may be present in any object, or they may only occupy the position of an influence, as when an African says when he escapes from danger, "The soul of my father saved me." This tends to become pantheism—a deification of all nature. Such is the root idea of Mlungu of the Zulus; the father of the race of men among the Sillocks on the Nile ;† Loma of the Bongo ;‡ heaven fire or lightning of the Mitto,§ and the Lubare of the Lake region.‖ This is a comparatively late

* Rowley.   † Schweinfurth.   ‡ *Ibid.*   § *Ibid.*   ‖ Mackay.

development, and can only be elaborated after religion has passed through many phases, and man comes to regard the supernatural as distinct from and independent of his own will. The older forms may and do persist after philosophy has arrived at the pantheistic idea, but they are on the wane, and preparing to follow the systems which preceded into the land of forgetfulness. Before considering the doctrines of substitution, sacrifice and sacrificial worship, we may examine traces of nature-worship under the form of the creative or reproductive spirit, as that has survived in civilised lands in popular superstition, ceremonial acts, and national festivals.

One of the most familiar of festivals is the village May-pole, an undoubted survival from very ancient times. We may the better understand its significance if we compare the yearly merry-making on the village green with the Galla festival of Woda, or, better still, with the annual sacrifices to Tari by the Khonds of India. Our knowledge of this latter festival is full and accurate. Major MacPherson, who suppressed the custom now over forty years ago, wrote an account of it in all its details, of which what follows is a brief summary :—The sacrifices were intended to ensure good crops and avert accidents of all kinds in connection with the fertility of the soil and yield of crops, as well as fecundity and productiveness among the people. The victim, or Meriah, was acceptable to the goddess only in the event of being purchased or being born of a victim purchased at a previous time. To avoid accidents or difficulty in procuring a suit-

able Meriah at the time of the festival, a number
were always kept on hand to be ready in case of
emergency. Of these, many were women, and, as
the victims could not be sacrificed if pregnant, many
of them managed to escape their fate for years.
Their children were, however, doomed as victims
from infancy, as were also children of a free woman
by a male Meriah. Even free people, Khonds themselves, at times sold their children as victims. To
sell a son or daughter was the highest virtue, as
"the child died that all the world might live." *
These ghastly sacrifices were offered by tribes and
sub-tribes, and were so arranged that each house-
holder got a shred of flesh to sow in his fields about
the time when the crop was laid down, or as the
corn already in the earth began to sprout.

The sacrifices were performed in the following
manner :—Ten days before the festival the victim's
hair was cut off. Thereafter came days of feasting,
dancing, and devilry. On the day preceding the
sacrifice the victim was dressed in new and very
fine garments, and then led from the village in
grand procession, with every possible circumstance of
display and honour. With music, dancing, exuberant merriment, and homage done to the victim,
the procession wended its way to the sacred grove,
at a distance from any dwellings, none of the
trees of which might be felled or touched with an
axe. Arrived at the grove, the victim was tied to a
post, anointed with a mixture of oil and turmeric,
and richly adorned with cut flowers. During the

* MacPherson.

whole of that day a species of reverence equivalent
to adoration was paid to the Meriah. There was a
constant struggle to obtain a flower, a particle of
the turmeric, even a spittle from the victim's person,
and these were regarded as sovereign and absolute
in all cases to secure the end sought by the worshipper. On the day of sacrifice the dance was
continued till noon, when it ceased, and the assembled crowd—for young and old were present—proceeded to the final act. The victim was again
anointed as before, and at times carried in triumphal
procession from house to house. At this stage the
Meriah might not be bound nor make any sign of
resistance. It was indeed essential that there should
be a voluntary surrender and sacrifice. To ensure
success and perfect obedience with apparent willing-
ness, the priests might, and often did, break the
bones of both arms and legs, or, when this was not
done, they gave a dose of some narcotic, as opium.

The method of putting the victim to death was
strangulation, and that was performed in the following manner :—A green branch from a tree was
cleft for a length of a few feet, and the victim's
neck inserted into the fork thus formed, after which
the officiating priest closed and secured the free
ends. He then wounded the Meriah slightly with
his axe, when the crowd rushed forward with knives
and bill-hooks to tear the flesh from the bones in
shreds and fibres, leaving the head, thorax, and
abdomen intact. An alternative method was to
fasten the victim to the trunk of a wooden elephant
which revolved on a pivot. As it whirled round

and round the crowd cut strips of flesh from the living Meriah. In each case the flesh was treated in the manner we shall presently see. In one district the method of death was slow roasting before a large fire. In this case a low stage was formed and on it the victim was placed. Fires were lighted and burning brands applied to make the sacrifice roll and wriggle as long as possible. The more the victim rolled, and the more tears and cries, the more plentiful would be the crop.

All this looks like a sacrifice to the goddess Tari, but when the treatment of the victim while held captive, and the homage paid before being put to death, together with the use made of the shreds of flesh is considered, it is highly probable that the intention was the sacrifice of the goddess herself; the decaying powers of nature put to death in order that the spirit of these powers might re-enter the earth as a creative and reproductive power, in the same manner as the spirit of the slain king entered his successor and dwelt there. Confirmation of this view is derived from the manner in which the flesh was disposed of, which was as peculiar as it is suggestive.

The strips and shreds of flesh cut from the Meriah were instantly carried away by appointed persons to the several villages represented at the festival and sacrifice. To secure prompt arrival, relays of runners were posted at short intervals along the roads. Arrived at the village, the runner deposited the flesh in the place of public assembly, and there the priest divided it into two portions.

One portion he buried in a hole in the ground, to
which, while he performed the operation, he kept
his back carefully turned. Then each villager, all
having rigidly fasted till now, added a little earth
till the hole was filled up. The other portion of
flesh the priest divided among heads of families,
who wrapped up each his share in green leaves and
proceeded at once to bury it in their corn-fields.
"For three days no house was swept, and silence
was generally observed."* In three days corn
sown sprouts ; so, too, by inference, the spirit of corn
represented by the Meriah. The head and entrails
of the victim, which, as we have seen, had been left
intact, were watched by the priests for a night, and
next day burned with a whole sheep, and the ashes
scattered over the fields.

These observances clearly show that power was
ascribed to the victim other than is associated with
sacrifice to secure the favour of deity. But it may
be objected that there is no connection between such
bloody rites as those represented by Khond sacrifices and the merry-making on fine summer morn-
ings, as ruddy youths and fair maidens dance around
the village May-pole. To trace that connection we
must go back to a time when May-day festivities
meant, not the exuberant energy and frolic of
youth, but the stern realities of a religion observed
by men in terrible earnest, and accompanied by the
sacrifice of quivering human beings to secure life and
favour from the gods. In order to understand this
we must trace briefly the history of another form

* Campbell.

of sacrifice and development of divinity common among the Celtic tribes of Europe.

The story of the death of Balder, the good and beautiful god, is familiar to all readers of Professor Rhys' *Celtic Heathenism*. The goddess Frigg obtained an oath from fire, water, metals, trees, beasts of all kinds, birds, and creeping things, that they would not touch or injure Balder. When this was done the god was regarded as invulnerable and immortal. Loke, the evil-worker, was displeased at what Frigg had done, and sought to discover if anything had been omitted from the oath by which he could injure or kill the god. He discovered that the mistletoe had not been included, as being too young to swear. So Loke went and pulled the mistletoe, which he brought to the assembly of the gods. A twig of it was given to Hödur, who made it into an arrow, which he shot at Balder. It pierced him through the heart and he fell down dead. The assembled gods stood speechless for a great space, and then lifted up their voices and wept, for the best and bravest had fallen. Then Balder's ship was launched by a giantess who came riding on a wolf, and his body placed on board on a funeral pile. When his wife Nanna saw what was done her heart burst for sorrow and she died. Her body was laid beside her husband, and so too were his horse and trappings. The ship having been fired, was sent to sea with its sad freight, and so ended the life of Balder. This is briefly the story which in the original Edda is told with great amplification of circumstance. Its very minuteness suggests that it belongs to that class of myths which are invented to explain ritual ; for a myth is never so graphic as when it is a transcript of what the narrator has seen.[*] The main incidents are : first. the pulling of the mistletoe ; and secondly, the death and burning of the god. Both these incidents appear to have formed an essential part of Celtic observances, as cut flowers and the death of the Meriah did of the ritual of the Khonds. We may now turn to May-day customs.

In all parts of Europe the peasantry, from time immemorial, have been in the habit of kindling fires and performing ceremonial acts on certain days of the year. It is a universal custom to dance round Midsummer fires, leap over them, and treat them as in a manner sacred. These customs can be traced back to the time of the Druids. They, in various forms, survived all and every change, and still persist, though thousands of years have elapsed since the reasons which gave them birth have passed away from the public mind. In Caithness, within the last seventy years, each family in the neighbourhood of Watten carried bread and cheese, before sunrise on May morning, to the top of a hill called Heathercow, and left it there.[†] After sunrise the cowherds might take away the spoil for their own use. No one could explain the origin of the practice ; it was unlucky to neglect it, that was all. Here we have a survival of an offering to the earth goddess, which in Druidical times was accompanied

* J. G. Frazer.   † Rev. A. Gunn, MS. Notes.

with bloody rites and sacrifices, in which the sacred mistletoe played an important part. It seems to carry us back to the days of Balder, when men killed the spirit of vegetation and creative energy in the person of their god, that it might re-enter the growing corn and make the earth fruitful once more. In the Western Isles the people on a given day poured out libations to the sea-god Shony, and then held a festival with curious rites, which were observed not more than two centuries ago. There is an account of the practice, written about 1690, as performed at that date, and with which the writer seems to have been familiar :—" The inhabitants of this island (Lewis) had an ancient custom to sacrifice to the sea-god called Shony at Hallowtide, in the manner following. The inhabitants round the island came to the Church of St. Malvay, having each man his provision along with him ; every family furnished a peck of malt, and this was brewed into ale. One of their number was picked out to wade into the sea up to the middle, and, standing still in that posture, cried out with a loud voice : ' Shony, I give you this cup of ale, hoping that you'll be so kind as to send us plenty of sea-ware for enriching our land for the ensuing year ;' and so threw the cup into the sea. At his return to the land, they all went into the church, where there was a candle burning upon the altar ; and then, standing silent for a time, one of them gave a signal at which the candle was put out, and immediately all of them went to the fields, where they fell a-drinking their ale, and spent the remainder of the night in dancing, singing, &c."* One would very much like to know what the worthy chronicler meant to convey by " &c.," and whether here, as in savagedom generally, the worship of Venus formed an essential part of the ceremony as performed at that time. He does tell us that the reformed pastors had spent years trying to suppress the practice, but with indifferent success. Corresponding acts of devotion, now represented by ceremonial usages, were performed by the Celts in early spring and at Midsummer.

Similar customs are common in every country in Europe. For example. In Bohemia the Spring Queen is dressed with garlands and crowned with flowers. She then, accompanied by a band of girls, who whirl round her continually, singing as they go, proceeds from house to house announcing that spring has come, and wishing them the blessings of the year. " In Ruhea, as soon as the trees begin to grow green in spring, the children assemble on Sunday and go out into the woods, where they choose one of their playmates to be the Little Leaf Man. They break branches from the trees and twine them about the child till only his shoes peep out from the leafy mantle. Singing and dancing, they take him from house to house asking for gifts of food. Lastly, they sprinkle the Leaf Man with water, after which they feast on the food they have collected." † A somewhat similar custom is observed in England, where a chimney-sweep walks about encased in holly and ivy, and accompanied by his

---

* Martin. † J. G. Frazer, quoting Mannhardt.

fellow-craftsmen, who collect money with which to have a carouse.

These customs, which might be illustrated indefinitely, are all analogous to the setting up and decoration of the village May-pole. Formerly it had to be renewed from year to year, the carrying of the new pole into the town being accompanied by crowds in holiday attire, who kept up a continual singing and clapping of hands with whirling and dancing. The object of the custom undoubtedly was to bring in the fructifying spirit of vegetation newly awakened, and for this purpose a newly cut pole and freshly gathered flowers were necessary. As the ancient Druidical sacrifices were abolished under the influence of an advancing conception of divinity, the festivals remained, merely changing their outward form and expression. What was stern reality became a pleasant pastime, and so came to be continued through the centuries, after men had forgotten the object served by them in a ruder age. And this affords an illustration of how among a savage people customs change so slowly. Two or three generations of literature do more to change thought and obliterate myth than thousands of years of tradition. Hence it is that in Africa, Australia, parts of India, and the South Sea Islands, we have at present time conditions similar to what obtained in Europe long before the rise of the Greek Republic. From this long digression we must now return to the consideration of African sacrifices, substitutionary and propitiatory.

CHAPTER IV

SACRIFICE

WE have already seen that the earliest form of human sacrifice was associated in the minds of men with killing the god himself. The divine King of Congo was put to death by his successor. In the Fiji Islands old people are burned alive. When a king of Kabonga is near his end the magicians quietly strangle him. Certain tribes of East Africa put their kings to death as soon as wrinkles or grey hairs appear.* A modification of the custom of king-killing was introduced when the expedient of temporary kings was reached. These could be put to death at stated intervals. We have met with examples of this in Sofala and Calicut. Ancient Babylonia affords another illustration. There, when the time drew near that the king should be put to death, he abdicated for a few days, during which a temporary monarch reigned and suffered in his stead. "A prisoner condemned to death was dressed in the king's robes, seated on the king's throne, allowed to issue whatever commands he pleased, to eat, drink, and enjoy himself, and to lie with the king's concubines. But at the end of the

* Isaacs, *Travels and Adventures in East Africa.*

five days he was stripped of his royal robes, scourged and crucified." * This same custom, softened down, is observed in Cambodia, where the king abdicates annually for a few days. The substitute performs all functions of State, and receives the revenues for the time he reigns. At the close of his brief term of office he goes and does homage to the king, and then, as his last act, orders the elephants to trample the "mountain of rice." This is a large scaffold hung round with rice-sheaves. When they are trampled down the people gather up the rice, each man taking home a portion to mix with his seed-corn and so secure a good harvest.†

Once the idea of substitution was reached, sacrifice as an institution would develop rapidly, and the curious thing is, that a trace of the original system of killing the god has remained to tell the world of an older and ruder conception of divinity. To the ancient man-god it was so convenient to have another take his place, that we can fancy the innovation being hailed with joy by the ruling castes, who by it were freed from the uncertainties of popular discontent and the accidental advent of signs of decay. But the doctrine of substitution had its disadvantages, and these in course of time would be felt and have far-reaching effects. Under the old order men were accustomed to offer homage to the living king; and their supreme and final act of worship was when he was put to death that his spirit might enter his successor as the creative, fructifying and preserving power of the world.

* J. G. Frazer, quoting Athenæus. † Aymonier.

Worshippers who associated such ideas with sacrifice could not be prevented from viewing the real victim offered, even as a substitute, as in some sort divine by inherent right. If divine by inherent right, the question of the spirit's return to the real king might be raised. Advanced thinkers would ask whether the spirit of the god, or the god-life, left the king to enter the substitute, slave or criminal, when the former abdicated, and if so, whether other causes might not lead to the same result? Could a successful revolt, headed by a bold and fearless man, secure to the usurper the god-life the moment the king was deposed or slain? If so, revolt and revolution might be, if not lawful, at all events possible, without the collapse of the world. Again, was there a true transference of divinity to the temporary king, his mean and common spirit taking the place of the god in the hereditary monarch? If so, might not men of ambition become substitutes, and at the last act rally their friends in order to retain the divine spirit permanently? Would the substitute's spirit, which dwelt in the king, give place to the returning god-spirit, "poor fluttering thing," after the victim was slain? With such questions pressing for solution—and for a question to be raised among savage men is to find an answer—kings and their advisers would naturally seek to foster faith in an hereditary principle of divinity apart from the actual sacrifice of the god himself. We call this the divine right of kings. When this conception of hereditary divinity was reached, men would sacrifice to the king-god as a personal and hereditary spirit—a spirit dwelling

in the king in virtue of his office, or whom he represented to men—rather than to the spirit of creative
and reproductive energy and vegetation which, in
an earlier and ruder age was undoubtedly the
savage's conception of his divine king. He was
divine, not because he was a personal immortal
spirit, but because in him was contained that spirit
or power which ensured the orderly continuance of
the course of nature.

The sacrifice made in former days of the king
himself by the priests, would, under the advance of
thought, be made in the first instance to the king,
and the more costly the sacrifices, and the more
elaborate the ritual, the greater would be the virtue,
and by consequence his influence and power. Kings
attaining to great eminence as conquerors and
administrators would be greatly honoured with
sacrificial offerings during their lives, and revered
after their death. Their successors, especially if
weaker men, would, in order to secure the continued
allegiance of their people, pay respect to their
memory. This, without any revolution of thought,
would take the form of offerings, prayer, and sacrifice. Then the spirit of the departed king visited
his successor in dreams and visions. At such times
he entered his person ; hence the common saying,
" He got the spirit of his father." By such means
he kept his successor informed of his wishes, which
were respected and obeyed ; thus enabling a weak-
ling to retain power which otherwise would have
dropped from his nerveless grasp. That this is no
phantasy is clearly proved by beliefs common among

Africans at the present day. A Kaffir who has a remarkable dream will begin to tell it next day by saying : "My father's soul was within me last night." Prophets claim to be god-possessed, or, in other words, to have within them the souls of departed priests or chiefs. In this case they work themselves into, or through long practice assume, a state of semi-coma. During their paroxysms and the succeeding unconsciousness they are treated as objects of worship ; in other words, they are truly divine for the time being.

Let us now proceed to illustrate these general statements by an examination of the sacrificial system common throughout the continent, and in doing so it will be well to select a few places, widely apart, as typical illustrations. The natives of South Africa discontinued human sacrifices before they had much contact with Europeans, and, being of mixed origin, we study their religious institutions at a disadvantage. But an examination of their system of thought leads us up to a time when their rites and sacrifices differed in no essential from what is common to the vast majority of the tribes inhabiting the continent, from 10° of north latitude to the farthest promontory of the south.

When the course of nature is not to a Kaffir's mind, as during drought, floods, sickness among men or cattle, misfortune in war, failure in hunting or a visitation of locusts, he offers propitiatory sacrifices to the offended deities. Each man sacrifices to his own ancestors ; each clan, through the magician, to the heads of the clan ; the tribe to the ancestors of its chief; but in the latter case the sacrifice can only be offered by the tribal priest, or by the chief in those rare instances in which he is not only the ruler but the high priest also. I am not aware of any ruler at present in South Africa being his own high priest, but the combination is not unknown. The chief Makoma used to offer the sacrifices on important occasions himself.

Here we have the curious anomaly of sacrifices to minor divinities made by ordinary householders, while those to superior deities can only be offered by the high priest if they are to be acceptable to the god. Those whose function it is to stand between men and the unseen, approach divinity with an offering for men's sins. They stand there as representatives or substitutes, taking the place of the worshippers. For a tribal offering may be made by the priest without a muster of the tribe or even the army. The sacred functions belong to sacred persons, and they determine how and when these are to be performed, and only obey certain general principles, without which no sacrifice is a genuine offering. One of these is that all sacrifices must be made by fire. Unless portions of the animal slain are burned, there has been no true offering, and the gods view the whole ceremony in grief and anger. Another is, that the animal must be honestly come by. A man may purchase a sacrifice, but this is rare, and, I think, regarded as irregular; but no man would sacrifice a beast that had been stolen. The most acceptable sacrifice is that which is a man's very own. There is also one phrase in the dedicatory prayer which is never omitted. It is this : " We do not offer the dead ; it is blood. We offer life. Behold, O ye hosts." During the time when the sacrifice is offered the priest stands as intercessor for the people in room of the chief. His orders are obeyed as the chief's, and his deliverances accepted as the very oracles of God.

It may at first sight be difficult to connect this doctrine of propitiatory sacrifice with that of substitution, as we have seen that in the case of the killing of the temporary king. And if this propitiary system of sacrifice were our only guide, it would be impossible to do so. But there is another system, complete in all its parts and distinct from the idea of propitiation, observed by the same people alongside of this doctrine. It is that of thank-offering and sacrificial thanksgiving. For every supposed benefit a man makes a thank-offering. It may be but a single grain of corn, or even an article of no value, as a tuft of grass, but it is never omitted. When a father offers a sheep as a thank-offering for the birth of a child, his idea is not only to recompense the soul of his father for good offices by so much burning fat, but to "give to those who were before" the keeping of the child's soul ; giving the soul to them in homage and thankfulness. This is undoubtedly the dedicatory offering of the soul by the sacrifice of a sheep as a substitute for the firstborn, a custom with which we are only too familiar elsewhere. Besides, the first child of a widow who re-marries, should her husband have fallen in war, is put to death : offered to the gods

as " the child of the assegai." * In making thank-
offerings for good offices a man adds to the portion
of the sacrifice that is burned something from his
own person, and men have been known to cut off a
finger or toe for this purpose, to enhance the value
of the offering. The Israelitish practice of shaving,
as a sign of having made a vow or formed a resolve,
is not unknown.† Adopting peculiar garments as a
head-dress, in token of anything remarkable having
happened to a man, is common.

When a tribe is at war, or preferably before
entering upon hostilities, if an enemy can be caught
he is put to death. The warriors eat his heart
raw.‡ Various parts of his body, supposed to be the
seat of particular virtues, are used in the preparation of the compound known as war medicine,
while shreds of fat from his kidneys are burned in
the fire. Much the same is done in the case of a
slain enemy who has distinguished himself for
bravery and feats of strength.§ This, though the
people do not say so, is undoubtedly an offering
made to the gods. The explanation given is, " Our
people always did so," and that war medicine, without the fat burning in the fire while it is being
prepared, would not act.‖ For the true significance
of such acts we must seek an explanation, not from
the people, who can give none, but from analogy,
and their resemblance to other acts performed by
the same people, or by others having customs in
common with them. The fat burned in the fire

---

* J. Sutton, MS. notes.   † Ibid.   ‡ G. M. Theal, Boers and Bantu.
       § Ibid.   ‖ J. Sutton, MS. notes.

when oxen are sacrificed in time of war, drought, or
the great annual festival of firstfruits, is avowedly
a gift to the gods,* the odour of which they inhale ;†
and when we find the burning of human fat in
almost identical circumstances—*i.e.*, war—and the
preparation of a magic decoction into which calcined
human flesh largely enters, and on which depends
its efficacy, the conclusion is forced upon us that
here we have the last lingering traces of human
sacrifice. Nor is this the only use made of portions
of the human body in connection with the religious
ritual of the people. The dried fingers of a man's
hand is an essential portion of a magician's outfit
when he goes to curse his chief's enemies.‡ Wizards
deal largely in human flesh.§

The multiplication of sacrifices is acceptable to all
the gods ‖ of heathendom, and one case is on record
in which tribes killed every hoof of cattle and
destroyed every peck of corn to secure the favour of
their ancestors. True, the priest who ordered this
to be done promised that there should be a general
resurrection of both ancestors and cattle on a given
day, that of full moon ; but this only adds to the
completeness of the faith reposed in his predictions
as the oracles of God. On the appointed day
thousands of men and women gathered for a moon
dance ; folds had been erected for the cattle that
were to rise ; stores for the corn which men were
to gather ; houses for the ancestors who were to
come clad in armour. In honour of the great event

---

* Chalmers, J: Sutton, Hon. C. Brownlee.   † Chalmers.
‡ Hon. C. Brownlee, *Christian Express.*   § Dr. Elmslie, MS. notes.
‖ J. Sutton, MS. notes.

the sun was to rise double on the resurrection morning. During that night sounds of revelry were
heard far and near, but when day came the sun rose
alone while his companion lagged behind. Black
fear entered every heart. Starvation stared men in
the face. Umlanjeni declared they had mistaken
the day of full moon, and urged a resumption of the
dance with assured triumph on the morrow. But
men had no heart left, and the next twenty-four
hours were but a sorry time. Once more the sun
rose in lonely majesty, and men's worst fears were
realised ; the gods had betrayed them. By such
experiences did men learn to differentiate the natural
and supernatural.

When a chief dies, one at least, or it may be
many persons are put to death for having killed
the king by the exercise of the unlawful art of
witchcraft ; but this falls rather under magic and
divination than under sacrifice. The only connection it has with the latter is, that among most
tribes the chief is never allowed " to go alone." A
few of his wives, servants and slaves must be killed
to accompany him and attend to his wants. It
may also be noted that the ruling chief may order,
even in the case of accusations of having caused his
father's death, the substitution of an ox for the
condemned person.* The ox is sacrificed, not killed,
as a criminal substitute for the wizard, who is set at
liberty. This seems to point to the victims of
witchcraft, whom we generally regard as criminals
under native law, being in reality a sacrifice to the

* Hon. C. Brownlee, MS. notes.

gods. The substitution of an animal, which is killed
as a sacrifice, is common in cases where the patient
has recovered, though causing sickness with intent
to kill is a capital crime.

When we leave South Africa and pass into the
Lake region all doubt about substitutionary human
sacrifice is set at rest. If a Wayao murderer is
caught he may make compensation by giving a few
slaves to be put to death, so that they may accompany the murdered man, taking his place to attend
upon him.* Should the murderer escape, one of his
relatives is caught and treated as if he were the
murderer. The object here is not so much the
punishment of crime as an offering to the deceased,
whose spirit would naturally be enraged at his own
relatives were they not to pay due honour to it by
sending, either the murderer to be his slave, or such
of his relatives or slaves as may make amends for
his absence. Of departed spirits some have considerable influence among the gods. Matanga of
the Wayao has many powerful servants, and ar-
ranges most of the details of the spirit world in
that region.† He is capricious and easily offended,
but can be coaxed by judicious flattery. Men having
ghostly relations with him, or with lesser divinities
through him, can compound for personal service by
substitution. So, instead of betaking themselves to
the land of shades, as in duty bound, when a relative to whom they owe allegiance dies, they send a
number of slaves as their representatives to do duty
by proxy.

* Rev. Duff MacDonald. † *Ibid.*

But it is when we enter the territories of powerful kings, like Mr. Stanley's friend Mtesa, that we
can study primitive sacrificial institutions to best
advantage.   Broken and scattered tribes like those
round Lake Nyassa, or bands of marauding warriors
like the ancestors of the tribes inhabiting South
Africa, do not retain the institutions of their forefathers in their unblemished splendour.   In the one
case, poverty, oppression, and the constant fear of
death or captivity, slowly but surely undermine and
modify original institutions.   In the latter, daring
warriors learn by degrees to defy even the gods, or
at least neglect them.   That stout old Roman who
threw the sacred chickens into the sea was not a
bolder reformer than the Zulu monarch who gave
battle to the army of Moselekatse when all the
omens of heaven and earth warned him of defeat.
More fortunate than the Roman, a decisive victory
saved both his own head and his country's freedom.

Among the Wagogo the simplest form of human
sacrifice is when the magician comes to the palace
with two bunches of grass dipped in the blood
of a victim slain quietly and without ostentation.*
These he lays on the lintel or threshold, where they
are touched by the king, and so offered to the gods.
Of these gods the principal is Makusa, who, as we
have seen, claims a right higher than the king over
the Lake, as the embodiment of the powers of
nature.   He it is that is personified by the Lubare,
who is the real object of worship.   Makusa as a
sort of Neptune is but a chief Lubare.†   He enters

---

* Mackay, of Uganda.   † Felkin.

a person ; that person is god, and to him sacrifices
are offered. Closely bound up with the worship of
the Lubare is the care of the place where the king's
predecessors are kept, or rather of these predecessors
themselves, for the Lubare holds converse with the
dead as with the living.*

Associated with, or subordinate to the Lubare
are Nende, Kajangeyewe, and Kubuka, who are a
kind of national guardian spirits. These appear in
persons who are god-possessed, and such persons are
always accompanied by magicians, priests, and executioners ; † that is to say, those who slay victims for
the sacrifices. The god-possessed person has but to
demand a victim, when a wayfarer is caught, bound,
beheaded, and offered in sacrifice. Every person
holding the sacred office of priest or magician claims
to have the spirit of the king dwelling in him, or at
least visiting him at intervals.‡ The head wife
of every great man's harem is called " Kuda
Lubare " §—i.e., slave of the spirit, meaning one in
whom the god dwells. The same terms are applied
to the child of a woman long barren, and who
offered sacrifice and prayed to the Lubare for offspring. This is a true dedication of issue at the
shrine when the offering is made. Of this we have
an illustration, in widely different circumstances,
when Hannah said : " O Lord of hosts, if thou wilt
indeed look on the affliction of thine handmaid, and
give unto thine handmaid a man child, then I will
give him unto the Lord all the days of his life," ‖

---

* Felkin.   † Mackay, of Uganda.   ‡ Ibid.
  § Ibid.   ‖ 1 Samuel.

which vow Eli, worthy man, thought to be but the ravings of a drunken votary.

Mention has been made of the tombs of the king's predecessors. This is a large hut, of comparatively slight construction, and needing frequent repair or renewal. Connected with it is a large college of sorceresses, whose chief duty it is to tend the spirits of the departed and guard the sacred place. When the king decides that it must be repaired, he issues his orders to the members of this college, who see the work done, and report when it is completed. Offerings must now be made to their majesties as a kind of solatium for the trouble they were put to, owing to the disturbance in connection with the repair of their quarters. As many as two thousand victims have been offered on such occasions. These are to the Lubare as the earth god, rather than to the kings, for the Lubare is the genius of the country, the object of universal worship. So general is the worship of Lubare that no one leaves his hut in the morning without first throwing out an offering, as a wisp of grass, saying, " Here, Lubare, take that.*

To them Katonga, or Creator, and Lubare mean the same, for every phenomenon is subject to Lubare. Crops, famine, food, rain, thunder, storms on the lake, day, night; everything in nature has its Lubare, and still Lubare is one and not many. It is the spirit of Makusa, who is all and is every-where—a kind of universal deification of nature as animate. When sacrifices are offered to the Lubare,

* Mackay, Uganda.

as on the completion of repairs of the " house of
the king's ancestors " or the death of a great man,
the method of procuring victims is at once simple
and sufficient. If victims were selected by choice
from the sub-tribes and clans, difficulties of no
ordinary kind would be met with in the case of a
sudden demand for a parcel of five hundred or a
thousand ; if chosen by lot, expedients would be
adopted to avoid the ordeal. All these inconveni-
ences are avoided by the executioners, of which a
small army is kept, posting themselves on the great
highways approaching the capital and seizing
travellers on their way to the palace. At such
times the gods send the proper victims, and when a
sufficient number has been caught the sacrifices are
offered. These victims go as royal messengers,
or more properly pages, to attend on the king's
ancestors.

Turning to West Africa, where all religious institutions are modified by Fetish, the systems at
first seem distinct, not only in details, but in
original conception of what is due to divinity. A
closer examination shows that the conceptions of
Central and West Africa regarding the unseen
world are substantially the same, and that the
intention in sacrifice is the same. From killing the
god they passed to substitution, thence to propitiatory sacrifice and thank-offerings. Each kingdom
has its own particular customs and yearly festivals,
presenting an infinite variety of detail, but in their
general features the same ; marking the steady
advance of thought from the rude conceptions of

the days when the world was young, to a conception of divinity akin to Pantheism, and passing over into that system at various points.

In Gomba, when a sacrifice is offered, the victim is paraded about the streets after the manner of the Lord Mayor's show. He is decked out in finery, adorned with jewels, and wearing a crown and other insignia of royalty. From being a slave, he becomes something more than a king; he becomes a demi-god. He may do whatever he pleases and have all he fancies, should his tastes be like those of the damsel who asked the Baptist's head. Nothing is denied him, as long as it does not imply his escaping his doom at the appointed hour. As he parades the streets he receives and accepts the homage due to a god, and when slain, men prostrate themselves before the body. The body itself is taken up by the women, decorated and honoured as divine, and finally treated more as god than an offering to a god. The object seems to be, not so much an offering to the god as the killing of the god himself by substitutionary sacrifice. The King of Ashantee, when holding the great annual Fetish festival, calls it the festival of his fathers,* and is himself for the time regarded as the personification of the gods. His actions are not so much that of their delegate, which he claims at all times to be, but their actions, their words, and their very movements. If the king rises, the gods stand; if he reclines, they sleep; should he dance, they too caper about with the movements of his arms and legs. For the festival

* Ramseyer and Kühne.

he arrays himself with scrupulous care and with
extraordinary grandeur. Whatever of wealth and
splendour his palace holds is wrapped round his
person or attached to his garments. He is literally
loaded with precious gems and the most costly ornaments. The drums that are to accompany him in
procession are decorated with human skulls, while
soldiers, priests and executioners deck themselves
with what is acceptable to the gods and on which
they love to gaze. During the festival, sheep, goats,
and human beings are indiscriminately sacrificed. The
king, during the pageant procession, is carried by the
priests, and must on no account walk or even touch
the ground. He receives homage on behalf of his
fathers, and it is impossible to determine how much
the intention is to sacrifice to them or to the king
himself. They reside in him as the god in the
Fetish, and in virtue of such possession he is divine.

But the great festival of the year is the yam
festival. Before the day appointed for the king to
eat fresh yams there are processions, reviews, dances,
and general rejoicing, in which the king takes an
active part. On the fifth day of the festival a
human sacrifice is offered, or, to be correct, a
"messenger" is despatched by the king to the spirit
world. As this messenger is not designed for any
of his ancestors, nor charged with any commission
to them, the inference is that like the Khond sacrifices to Tari, the sacrifice is to the world of life and
reproduction. After the sacrifice is made, the king
eats fresh yams from a dish held by the chief cook,
who keeps stirring the contents with a gold fork,

while the nobles stand before him uncovered.* At
this and the palm-wine festival the honours of
adoration are all done to the king, and the progress
of the festival is consecrated by any stray person
about the palace doors being seized and slain as an
act of reverence to his majesty.† The treatment of
such victims after execution is thus described by
Kühne, who frequently witnessed such scenes.

"One took a finger, another an arm or foot, and
whoever obtained the head danced in crazy ecstasy,
painted its forehead red and white, kissed it on the
mouth, laughing, or with mocking words of pity,
and finally hung it round his neck or seized it with
his teeth. Another took out the heart and washed
it, carried it in one hand and a loaf of maize bread
in the other, and walked about as if he were eating
his breakfast.

"In the evening they brought the skulls of their
most important enemies from the mausoleum at
Bantama, and placed them, in the stillness of the
night, in front of the Fetish. Among them was the
skull of Sir Charles Macarthy, kept in a brass basin
and covered with a white cloth. . . . . On the next
day all laws were abrogated, and every one drinking
freely was permitted to do what was good in his
own eyes. Even funerals were celebrated for those
who had suffered capital punishment."

Here we have, in the extreme west, the common
Pondo custom of the abrogation of all law at the
feast of firstfruits. From the last sentence, which
Kühne does not explain, it is to be inferred that

* Ramseyer and Kühne.   † *Ibid.*

holding funerals for persons executed is, according to Ashantee notions, the farthest extreme of license to which men can go.

The festival of Bantama affords the king an opportunity of sending a messenger to his fathers. He delivers his charge slowly and deliberately, as if giving a diplomatic commission, and then the executioners cut off the victim's head, a knife having been previously run through his cheek and left there. Should the king remember anything he wished to say after the victim is slain, he orders another to be brought, and sends him with a hurried postscript lest his ancestors should be offended at the matter not being referred to in the original communication.

Bantama is the resting-place or mausoleum of the departed kings, and when Kühne was in Ashantee there were fourteen of the king's predecessors within its walls. It is a long building, divided into small cells, each of which contains the skeleton of a king ;* the coffins containing these, as well as the skeletons themselves, being connected together with gold wires. Each cell contains such articles as the tenant loved best during his life. At the festival of Bantama the skeletons are placed on chairs in the audience hall to receive the royal visitor. This they do in the order of seniority. The king on entering offers each skeleton food, and as he does so, passing from one to another, the victim selected for each is decapitated in the approved manner by the executioners. During the succeeding night, and after the monarchs are returned to their cells and coffins,

* Kühne.

victims are slain at intervals by beat of drum or sound of horn. With the regularity of the minute-gun, the horn sounds a double blast, which means "death"; then three rapid blasts, which signify an order to cut off a victim's head; followed by one long blast to tell that the head has dropped. When the building needs repair, the king pays it a visit of inspection, after which the same ritual as we saw among the Wagogo is observed, the victims being counted by hundreds. Should the king dance with his wives, a messenger must be sent to his fathers to explain why he is at that particular time engaged in the light pastime.*

But it is not necessary to go so far afield as Ashantee to find illustration of messages being sent to the spirit world. My father, who over seventy years ago resided for some years in the Highlands of Perthshire, used to tell how at that time the people of Glenlyon and Glendochart charged their dying relatives with messages beyond the grave, and that people came long distances to ask, as an extreme favour, that their wishes should be made known " beyond " about certain particulars, one of the most common requests being to explain away shady transactions : " If you meet such an one, tell him how we are, and all that is going on. I gave every penny he left to his daughter. Mind you tell him the dun horse, which I kept to get a better price for, died." Such were the commis-sions entrusted to the dying by pious Calvinists as late as the second decade of the present century;

* Kühne.

commissions from which even elders of the kirk were not exempt. If this may happen in the green tree of Puritanism, what may not be done in the dry tree of Paganism.

In Dahomey the customs observed are in their main characteristics identical with those of Ashantee and other West African kingdoms. One peculiarity of Dahomeyan religion is—and in this, so far as I know, it is singular—that the Fetish priest is supposed to be able to visit the regions of the dead in *propria persona*, as the substitute or representative of the living, and there act for them as if they were themselves present in the land of shades.* For example, a man falls ill and believes that he is being warned by some ancestral spirit that his presence is required beyond the bourne. He consults the priest, who on receipt of a suitable fee agrees to descend and make reconciliation on his behalf, so that he may continue to enjoy the upper air for a further period. When this is done the patient recovers ; if not, he is killed by evil persons ; the spirits never called at all, for the intervention of the priest is, within limits, effectual in all cases when the matter is in the hands of the gods. But this leads us to the verge of the doctrine of devils, which is an advanced form of savage religious thought ; the worship of devils being a late development as compared with that of the beneficent gods. After spirits were multiplied, men, in seasons of drought and times of disaster and stress of circumstances, would endeavour to conciliate the demon that

* Winterbotham, Rowley.

brought calamity. Hence it is that demon worship
is always propitiatory, while the worship of the
gods is devotional and sympathetic, as in thank-
offerings and tokens of goodwill and fellowship
towards the unseen, whether regarded as personal or
as the earth-god, nature, the mother of all. When
a king of Dahomey dies he must enter the lower
world in such regal state as became his dignity
while he lived. The number of victims is almost
incredible in order to make a grand procession.
During his life he sends substitutes and messengers
to spirit-land on the most slender pretext, or on no
pretext at all.

Similar illustrations of the doctrine of substitution by sacrifice might be given from the observances of American Indians, South Sea Islanders,
ancient Mexicans, and the Teutonic peoples of
Europe. In tracing the system we have seen how
the original practice of killing the god, as the spirit
of vegetation and creative energy, passed into the
form of substitution. Even in propitiatory sacrifice
we see the same idea of the earth spirit reappearing
whenever we can catch a glimpse of society under
primitive conditions. Sacrifices to kings or Fetish
are more to the earth-goddess than to the object to
which they are immediately presented; that is, to
the powers of nature as in vegetation and reproduction generally. This points back to the time
when the divine element of natural force resided in
kings, and was sacrificed to ensure a new resurrection with the opening year. Our inquiry has led u
away from that original conception of primitive

man to a more elaborate system of thought, which, gradually expanding, included within its range factors and forces, spirits personal and impersonal, and conceptions of man himself, of which the earlier philosophy took no account. To understand the further development of human thought, and how spirits came to be classified as good and bad, we must consider the restrictions under which divine and sacred persons were placed, and the reasons for such restrictions so far as these may be discovered.

CHAPTER V

WE have already seen how the Mikado of Japan and the divine King of Laondo lived surrounded with safeguards and restrictions. The dangers to which souls are exposed have also been touched upon. We shall now consider how these were guarded, and the fresh dangers to which taboos gave rise as restrictions were multiplied.

To the savage, as we know him, the great danger of existence is witchcraft and the action of charms and spells; and to secure himself against these he adopts such precautions as the nature of the case suggests. But witchcraft itself is a system which must have had an origin, and developed, from one or more simple conceptions, to be an art practised by persons who claimed to have communication with the unseen world. With the art we generally associate the ideas of pure mischief, but it was capable of being turned to good account, and the Scotch witches who banned rats from farmers' barns were thought worthy of a night's quarters and a substantial honorarium for their service. It has been hastily inferred that they learned the art from ecclesiastics, who, with bell, book and candle could ban the devil himself; but it is far more likely that priests learned the art of banning from an older cult coming down from the ages before the Flood.

With great persuasion I once induced an old woman to repeat to me a form of words for the banning of rats, which she had learned from " a woman that had the second sight and could do things." It is many years since I heard the doggerel, and can remember but one sentence of it, which, wedged in between imprecations and curses, was, that they should " shed the hair off their skulls " if they did not betake themselves to other quarters. This freed the farmer of the pest, but unfortunately the same power could be turned against any one who offended the witch. She in that case brought an army of rats down upon him, " to eat his corn and cut his sacks, and teach him to rue the day that he shut his door on Shoanad." This I heard from a Morven woman nearly thirty years ago, when quite a boy. If Andrew Lang, who in those days was a frequent visitor at Ardtornish, had but known Gaelic, we should have had a store of legends, rhymes and charms preserved to us which are now finally lost. I have travelled in all parts of the Highlands of Scotland, but nowhere have I met with such variety and richness of legend and myth as along the shores of the Sound of Mull.

If men need to guard against witchcraft in Scotland, how much more necessary must it be to do so in savagedom. Lives of great importance to the community we may expect to find guarded with special care, in the same way as we guard royalty in Europe, from attack by evil-disposed persons, sane and insane. There are not only the dangers which may lurk unseen near at hand, but also unknown dangers from a distance, and which are associated with the arrival of foreigners. Besides, there are districts specially charged with such malign influences, and any one visiting these must be purged and purified before he has any communication with others. Thus the missionary New and his party were, on their return from Killimanjaro, sprinkled by a " professionally prepared liquor " on arriving on the borders of the inhabited country. This was done by the priest, and before they had had any communication with the tribe. In the Yoruba country there is a custom of keeping strangers standing outside the gate of the town till sundown, lest evil spirits should enter with them if admitted during the day.* In South Africa the traveller must halt at a distance from the " great place," and is invited to the chief's presence only after the magician has performed the necessary incantations. Dinka and Bongo tribes on the Nile, take the like precautions against the advent of evil spirits when visited by strangers.† The South Sea Islanders subject those landing on their shores to a process of purgation to expel any evil which may hang about them. These are all general precautions taken for the benefit of the community. But do what he may, the savage cannot absolutely exclude evil from the tribe. Spirits do enter in the most unexpected manner, and witches will prowl

* Hinderer.　　　　　　† Schweinfurth.

about and follow their unlawful calling while men sleep. So he takes special precautions to guard those whose lives are of great value; precautions which, in their own language, " cannot be taken for commoners."

The arts of witchcraft are so subtle that those marked for its victims can be affected through the food they eat, if the wizard can but get his fingers into it, or even see it; through articles taken from their persons, as cut nails, hair, arms, ornaments, saliva, and also through all those articles which sacred persons may not see or touch. Thus it happens that those whose lives are so guarded may not eat in public, nor must their food be seen except by trusted personal attendants. In Gondokoro a guest asked to a marriage sends a present of food, but it must be carefully covered with a napkin to protect it from the influence of wizards and witches,* through whom the whole bridal party might be affected. A Wanyoro will not return by the way he went; his very footprints may in the interval be bewitched. The King of Loango may not be seen eating or drinking, on pain of death. In Dahomey the same law exists, and Cameron in his walk across Africa paid men to let him see them eat or drink.

By judiciously extending these taboos life may be made a burden too grievous to be borne by the persons so guarded, and a day comes when, utterly wearied and goaded to madness, the king defies the gods and asserts his own independence. Such defiance is the herald of reform and a further advance

* Felkin.

of thought. Those having charge of sacred mysteries must adapt their teaching to the stern facts of life, and adopt such ritual as will be submitted to by those who have the civil power in their hands. And this illustrates a curious trait of religious life the world over, viz., that reforms are forced on sacred persons from without. From within it does not come. They cling to tradition and usage, and when a custom or dogma has outlasted its time, instead of boldly throwing it aside, an attempt is made to prop and buttress it up by fresh legislation and more extended ritual, till some one comes and shivers the structure, and it falls crumbling to dust and nothingness by its own weight.

But there is another side to this mystery of taboos, for if the sacred person must be guarded from harm from without, so must others be protected from receiving hurt from him. He is neither in heaven nor on earth, and it is men's interests that he should be suspended as evenly as may be between the two. His divinity will be injured by too much contact with earth and with men; but then this very divinity is a source of danger should men be brought, in the ordinary relations of life, into too close contact with him. He is a source of blessing under proper conditions, but let these be violated, and his divinity becomes a source of greatest danger; a fire which, if touched, will burst forth to scorch and burn. Should any one wear the Mikado's clothes without his leave, he would have swellings all over his body.* Nor is this

* Kaempfer.

confined to Japan. The following quotation from
J. G. Frazer, quoting the authority of W. Brown
and a Paheka Madri, illustrates the lengths to
which taboos were carried in New Zealand.

" It happened that a New Zealand chief of high
rank and great sanctity had left the remains of his
dinner by the wayside. A slave, a stout hungry
fellow, coming up, saw the unfinished dinner, and
eat it up without asking any questions. Hardly
had he finished when he was informed by a horror-
stricken spectator that the food of which he had
eaten was the chief's. . . . . 'No sooner did he
hear the fatal news than he was seized by the most
extraordinary convulsions and cramp in the stomach,
which never ceased till he died about sundown the
same day. He was a strong man, in the prime of
life, and should any one have said he was not killed
by the taboo of the chief, he would have been
listened to with feelings of contempt for his ignorance and inability to understand plain and direct
evidence.'" This is not a solitary case. Mr. Frazer
quotes several others, and in each case it is plain
the persons died of sheer fright, so all-powerful can
a fixed belief become among an ignorant and superstitious people.

With such results before his eyes, it is not to be
wondered at if we find the savage placing sacred
persons among the dangerous classes, and that he
should extend taboos to persons and things supposed
to be dangerous. Those who touch the dead are, in
New Zealand and Africa, unclean till purified by
magicians. Indeed, the rules of ceremonial purity

are so strict among some tribes that cases are on
record where men have killed their wives for
lying down on their mats at forbidden periods.*
Hence it is that at such times women are secluded,
as also after child-birth. In the former case they
may be even rolled up in mats and suspended as in
a hammock for a period of six or seven days, to be
unstrapped and conveyed to a stream of water for
necessary sanitary purposes.

"The rules of ceremonial purity observed by
divine kings, chiefs, and priests; by homicides,
women at child-birth, and so on, are in some
respects alike. To us these classes of persons appear
to differ totally in character and condition. Some
of them we should call holy, others unclean and
polluted. But the savage makes no such moral
distinction between them. . . . . To him they are
dangerous and in danger, and the danger in which
they stand and to which they expose others is what
we should call spiritual or supernatural—that is,
imaginary." † One of the substances most commonly tabooed by savages is iron. No iron may
touch a sacred person's body. He may die when
a simple incision might save his life, but the incision
must not be made. A Hottentot priest never uses
a knife in performing the operation of circumcision ;
he uses a sharp bit of quartz instead. Gold Coast
natives remove all iron from their persons when
consulting Fetish.‡ Scottish Highlanders never use
iron nails or hammers in making the fire-wheel

---

* *Journal Anthrop.* ix.　　　　† J. G. Frazer.
‡ C. J. Gordon Cumming.

apparatus for the celebration of certain Yule festivals ; they use wooden pegs and stone hammers
instead. The Jews used no iron tools in building
their Temple in Jerusalem, nor in making an altar.

The objection to iron arose in all probability when
the metal was new and scarce, and so regarded
with superstitious awe and reverence. But soon,
daring spirits like Lamech arose, who, defying
custom and taboo, and believing only in the strength
of his own arm and the trusty weapons his son had
forged for him, turned the dreaded metal to good
account. A substance charged with such power
that spirits could not endure it in their presence,
and before which kings might fall down dead, put
into men's hands a terrible weapon which could be
used with disastrous effects even against the gods
themselves. But if iron could be used against the
gods, they in turn could use it against evil-doers,
and the priesthood would not be slow in availing
themselves of so potent a weapon. Apart from its
obvious utility as an arm, when properly forged and
shaped, it would be regarded as having magic and
miraculous power, when properly used, for the expulsion of evil. And so we find iron, and the metals
generally, occupying a prominent place in the
superstitions of all countries. When a Scottish
fisherman hears "the unclean animal"—a pig—mentioned, he feels for the nails in his boots and mutters
" cauld iron." So, too, if one of the crew utters
certain oaths or curses when at sea. He bans the
devil of ill-luck and disaster by nailing a horse-
shoe, preferably that of a stallion, to the stern of

his boat. A Golspie fisherman a few years ago had a small boat with which he had an extraordinary run of luck in the prosecution of his calling. Inside the stem was nailed an entire horse's shoe, given to him by "a wise person" As he prospered his ambition grew till he purchased a larger boat, selling the small one and its belongings to a neighbour. From the first day he went to sea with his new boat luck forsook him, nor would fickle fortune be wooed. He bethought him of his horse-shoe, and went to his neighbour to demand restitution. This was denied, the new owner contending successfully that he had purchased the "boat and its gear." * To this day that man believes that to parting with an old shoe was due the entire failure of his season's fishing. Whether returning luck—for he still lives and prospers—had an educative effect upon his mind, I do not know.

Sutherlandshire crofters and cottars ban, or expel, the spirit of death from a house after one dies, by placing bits of iron in the meal chest, the butter jar, whisky bottle, and other articles of food, without which precaution they would speedily " go to rottenness and corruption." Whisky not treated so has been known to turn white as milk and curdle. Among savages iron is held in the same veneration. The Baralongs, who are famous smiths, regard the blacksmith's trade as a sacred art. Furnaces are placed at a distance from the houses, and none dare approach when the metal begins to flow, except those versed in the mysteries of the craft.

* Rev. A. Mackay, MS. notes.

But in Africa it is on articles from the person, or which have belonged to one regarded as sacred, that the greatest care is bestowed. This is common to the Zulu and the Dinka, to the Galla and Dahomeyan. We meet with it in every possible relation of life. For example, a young Zulu soldier, who was travelling to join his regiment with a companion, arrived at a village where they were to spend the night. They were directed to the "travellers' hut," where they found a mat such as natives sleep upon. The soldier took the mat and unrolled it, when, to his dismay, he found it contained head ornaments and other articles of female dress, such as is only used by the king's household. Seeing this, he rolled the mat up again and put it aside. It belonged to a girl of the king's harem, on her way to the capital, who had stayed there a few nights before. She had forgotten her mat and ornaments. On arriving at headquarters he was at once detailed for cattle-guard, but on his return in the evening he was met by a young man of his regiment, who told him his companion had been put to death, and that he was to be killed for having touched articles belonging to sacred persons.* He fled, but was overtaken and put to death. If touching ornaments is a capital offence, stepping over the head of a recumbent African is a yet more serious crime, if the sleeper be a person sacred in virtue of position or office. The head is peculiarly sacred, and to step over it is the most grievous offence that a man can commit, if it be not excelled in enormity by pulling his hair.

* Hon. C. Brownlee.

When this sanctity of the head and the consequent
difficulty of disposing of shorn locks is borne in
mind, it will be seen that the barber's vocation is,
if an honourable one, a dangerous office. Suppose
an artist is called to perform a necessary office for
his chief, whose ample locks have become too secure
a retreat for the colonies that take shelter under
them, he must be first purified with sprinkling, and
have the tools of his craft cleansed by the magicians. He then proceeds to the royal residence, and,
in presence of the king's guards and officers of State,
removes the mass close to the skull. If after the
operation the king takes a chill the poor barber is
accused of something more than neglect of duty :*
he bewitched the king, or he may have given a hair
to his friend the wizard to enable the latter to do
the evil deed. In either case the barber must
stand his trial, in the first case as a principal, in
the second as an accessory, and failing his divulging
the wizard's name, must take the consequences of
his guilt if the magicians decide the case as one of
bewitching.

But should he honestly perform his office and no
untoward events follow, there remains the difficulty
of disposing of the shorn locks. Burn them, says
common sense; but to the savage common sense
often is what the law was to the elder Weller, " a
hass." To burn shorn locks would be to invite all
the demons of a locality to secure and treasure up
the very essence they are in search of in the ascend-
ing smoke. To them the smell of burning hair or

* J. Sutton, MS. notes.

nail clippings is what the carcase is to the vulture.
Nor is it safe to keep them by one, for who can
guard against rats and white ants, not to speak of
accidents of fire, war, and theft. The only prudent
course is to bury them.* But how and where?
And here the sacred and lawful art of the magician
comes to the aid of the perplexed. Sacred spots
are set apart for such purposes—a kind of consecrated ground where the chief can bury his shorn
locks and cut nails, as well as dispose of other necessary superfluities in the most approved fashion
prescribed in Deuteronomy xxiii. 13; there as a wise
sanitary precaution; in Africa as a sacred function;
at the lowest as a precaution against the works of
the devil.

And here I may say that those who had charge
of my own youth were most remiss in a necessary
and most important particular, evidence of which I
have to go before any jury of Celts over seventy
years of age with. One of my earliest recollections
is having my hair cut by an itinerant tailor, who
combined the art of clothing one's limbs with that
of unclothing the head. I remember him still: a
gaunt, lean-looking man, with hollow eyes and a
sepulchral voice. When the operation was finished
he directed that the severed locks should be gathered
up and burned, because, should the birds—it was
spring-time, and the danger was real—get the
smallest particle, even a single hair, to build
their nests, I should be grey at twenty-one. This
he insisted upon with the strongest asseveration

* Livingstone.

of its truth ; while I, evil imp as I must have been,
gathered up a handful of hair, which I threw over
the window for the robins. The deed was done.
The artist stood aghast, and now, though a good
decade from the time when grey hairs should appear,
I carry the evidence of my own folly to kirk and
market.

The gods of the Dakota Indians are mortal, and
propagate their kind. Their Onkteri resemble a
bull, and can extend their tails and horns to the
sky, the seat of their power.* The earth is believed
to be animated by the spirit of the female Onkteri,
while the water and the earth beneath the water is
the abode of the male god. The Onkteri have power
to issue from their bodies an essence, signifying a
god's arrow, which can work wholesale destruction.†
The priests possess or claim all the power ascribed
to the gods, and are believed to pass through a
series of inspirations by which they receive the god-
spirit. They lay hold on all that is mysterious,
predict events, and declare that they bring about
events of which they made no prediction. They have
duplicate souls, one of which remains with the body,
while the other wanders at will. Clearly it is necessary that such persons should be surrounded by such
restrictions as will ensure the peace and safety of the
community. And so we find in Africa, America, Asia,
and the South Seas the same system of taboo ; the
same objections to certain objects and animals, and
the same sanctity of others, running into clan badges
and totems, which are at once sacred and to be cared

* Schoolcraft. † Bettany.

for, while they afford protection to those whose symbols they are.

But let men guard as they may ; let them surround divinities with restrictions, and take every precaution against evil persons getting possession of objects dangerous to their lives, accidents will happen and evils will accumulate, with a corresponding increase among those spirits who cause them. So, as we have a process of evolution going on among the gods, we have also a development of the doctrine of devils. This I do not propose to trace fully, but it is necessary to refer to the subject in general terms before we consider the methods adopted for their expulsion.

How man arrived at the idea of good and evil spirits as personal beings is impossible to determine with accuracy. It is probable after he reached the conception of a soul separate from the body, personal and immortal, or at least capable of existence in a distinct spirit-world, he began to attribute to such souls the same character as was borne by the man while he lived. The soul of a seditious man would foment sedition on earth among those whom he could influence after his death. So, too, the soul of a murderer, a thief, or a contentious man would incite to similar crimes. These would be regarded as evil spirits, to be dealt with as men of like disposition are dealt with. To secure society against their influence, only two ways were open to primitive man : one, to defy them, as is often done in the case of men of evil disposition, and so make them practically outcasts ; another to conciliate them, and so by acts of bribery and flattery secure their good offices, or at least their neutrality. Both these methods are found wherever savage man dwells. Devils are cursed, defied, expelled the country, and treated as we do our dangerous classes. At other times they are flattered, cozened, and feasted with sacrifice, in order that the largeness of the offering may be a sufficient inducement for them to refrain from evil. We shall in the present inquiry meet frequently with devil-worship, but here it may be well to inquire how primitive man sought to rid himself of spirits which he both feared and hated.

CHAPTER VI

EXPULSION OF DEMONS

WHEN man found his steps dogged by demons, he sought for means by which he could rid himself of those imps of evil which rendered his life an insupportable burden. His first impulse was to surround himself with safeguards, as a warrior in mail armour. But this necessitated an increase of restrictions each time evil spirits or daring men discovered means of breaking through his taboos. With the discovery of gunpowder mail armour became useless. Bullets could only be resisted by an increase in the weight and thickness of the protecting coat of mail, and warriors found it necessary to change their methods. So the savage whose taboos are rendered useless by a Lamech, finds it necessary to re-examine the whole surrounding. Must he add to the number of restrictions, to the weight of the already overburdened taboos, till they become like swaddling clothes in which he cannot move or breathe? Are his movements to be restricted as dangers multiply? Does the advent of each fresh enemy necessitate a re-adjustment of his whole philosophy?

The savage, feeling the awkwardness of his position by ever-increasing restrictions, arrived at the conception that, by a supreme effort made periodically,

or as occasion might arise, he could rid himself,
for a time at least, of the evils which surrounded
him.   And when we come to this doctrine of devils
and their expulsion, we arrive at a point which
marks a distinct advance in thought. Under the
earlier forms the king or earth spirit did good or evil
according to humour or caprice ; but with the conception of personal spirits, divided into a good class
and a bad, we find men projecting into the supernatural what they experienced in the natural world.
Their philosophy, crude as it was, was based on
observation, and embodied the results of experience
so far as savage man could formulate his experience
into a system. When taboos failed to meet the case,
men adopted the bolder policy of making war on
devils. Nor is the savage singular in the methods
adopted to expel evils. When fasts and prayers
failed the inhabitants of European cities in the
expulsion of the devils of epidemic diseases, they
made war upon them in sewers and cellars, and
to far better purpose than by the older and more
pious method of priestly intercession. A comparison
of the methods adopted for the expulsion of evils in
Africa, and survivals amongst ourselves, gives one
the impression that popular imagination is not yet
far removed from the age of Balac, whose only hope
lay in having a powerful magician, like the prophet
Balaam, to curse his enemies before he joined his
forces in battle with theirs.

Taking South Africa—with the practice of which
I was long familiar—first, it may be said in a general
way that no " commoner " dare interfere with spirits

either good or bad, beyond offering such sacrifices
as are sanctioned by custom. Demons may haunt a
man, and render his life a burden, but he must
submit to their machinations until the case is taken
in hand by the proper authorities. A baboon may
be the messenger of evil spirits, and perch itself on
a tree within easy gunshot, or regale itself in his
maize field ; but to pull a trigger at the brute would
be worse than suicide. As long as the man remains
a solitary sufferer he has little chance of redress. It
is assumed, he has been guilty of some crime, and
that the ancestors have in their wrath sent the
demon to torment him. But should his neighbours
suffer ; should the baboon from choice or necessity—
for men do pluck up courage to scare the brutes—
select a fresh field in which to glean its supper, or
another man's barn roof for its perch, the case alters
its complexion. The magicians now take the matter
up seriously. One man may be visited by the
ancestors with severe reproof, as being haunted by
a demon, but a whole community is another matter.
Clearly in that case there is something amiss, and a
remedy must be found. To shoot the baboon will
not serve the purpose. African spirits are not amenable to powder and lead, as Scottish witches are to
powder and silver bullets, and to kill the baboon
would only be to enrage the demon and increase the
danger. The first thing to do is to discover where
the devil has his permanent abode. This is generally
a deep pool of water with overhanging banks and
dark recesses. There the villagers gather with
priests and magicians. Under the direction of their

ghostly counsellors, and secured from harm by their presence, men, women, and children pelt the demon with stones. Drums are beaten and horns blown at intervals, and when all are worked up into a frenzy of excitement, as one after another catches a glimpse of the imp as he tries to avoid the missiles, he takes his flight at a single bound, and the village is free from his influence for a time. Baboons may now be killed and crops protected. While the stone throwing goes on, all present, and especially the women, hurl the most abusive epithets at the object of their fear and vengeance.

There is no periodic purging of devils, nor are more spirits than one expelled at a time. I have noticed frequently a connection between the quantity of grain that could be spared for making beer, and the frequency of gatherings for the purging of evils and other necessary purposes. No large gathering can be held in Africa without feasting and drinking, especially the latter. Like the Scotch factor, anxious to let a barren moor with hardly a feather on it, to an Englishman, as " one of the finest bits o' ground i' the north," and who after the second tumbler of " toddy," suggested a third before closing the bargain, on the ground that " it's dry wark talking," the African finds all public functions, even his devotions, " dry wark," and needs his pombe. If this is not to be had, the assured result is failure.

There are demons who are not amenable to stone-throwing and abuse. Such methods would only give them further opportunity for mischief by an increased knowledge of village affairs. They in that case could

adapt their methods to the new conditions, and the
end of that place would be worse than the first, for
they would enter it clean swept of all effectual means
of defence.   So the Dinka and Bongo expel their
devils by guile.* There the exorcist begins by
holding a conversation with the demon. He ascertains his name ; how long he has been there ; where
he belongs to ; his permanent residence ; kinsfolk,
acquaintances, and other particulars, all the while
disguising his own identity as a devil-doctor. When
he ascertains all he wishes to know, he hurries to the
woods to collect such medicines as are effectual for
the expulsion of demons of the class to which the one
in question belongs.   After this his course is clear :
he sends the evil one beyond the bounds of his
diocese by bell, book, and candle, or, to be literal,
by horn, calabash, and torch.

The Wazeramas, more tender of heart towards
their demons, expelled them by gentler means than
a shower of. stones or a drastic purge.   Suppose a
patient is devil-possessed, he is taken out of his hut
and propped up against a tree in presence of the
assembled villagers.   An ancient crone ladles out
beer to all who wish a draught.   When she has
completed her round of the crowd, drums are beaten,
horns blown, and all manner of musical instruments
played.   The demon, captivated by the music, has
his senses—"'cuteness"—dulled for the time, and at
the auspicious moment, when the noise has reached
a maddening pitch, the magician entices him to enter
a stool, wooden pillow, or any other object that can

* Schweinfurth.

be easily carried about.* This he conveys to a safe place, where he can deal with the demon at will and prevent his re-entering the patient. He, poor beggar, standing on one leg propped against the tree, is either killed outright by noise and excitement, or by a process of reaction obtains sleep, and frequently recovers within a few days or even hours.

When a Galla exorcist is called upon to exercise his powers over the unseen world, against any one of the eighty-eight demons that haunt the tribe,† he kills a goat, the entrails of which he hangs about his neck. Thus arrayed, he carries in one hand a bell, which he rings " to waken the demon," and in the other a whip. After he has capered about for a time ringing his bell, he suddenly raises his whip, with which he gives the patient several sharp cuts. The demon, not liking such treatment, takes to his heels; a final flourish of the whip in the air as the demon flies past completes the process, and the magician goes his way carrying his fee along with him, which is the only guarantee against the demon's return. I recommend this method to European physicians whose accounts are of long standing !

Of all methods employed for the expulsion of evil spirits that found among the Wanika is the gentlest I have met with. There they are treated with the care and consideration with which ladies of quality were treated when they walked abroad a century ago. This method may be illustrated by taking the case of a patient who is devil-possessed, as has been done with the preceding. A mortar filled with water

* J. Thomson.   † Krapf.

is placed at his bedside. Next a gaudily-coloured
stick, richly ornamented with beads, bits of glass,
and ornaments, is stuck in the ground close at hand.
A boy dips a bundle of twigs in the water, with
which he sprinkles the head of the patient. The
people beat drums, dance, sing, and play as if round
a May-pole. The demon loves music, and he loves
beads and gewgaws. As the merriment proceeds he
thinks people are off their guard, and he looks at
the stick. As he looks he becomes fascinated and
leans towards it. Finally, he leaves the patient and
enters the stick, when it is promptly pulled from the
ground by the magician.* What he does with the
demon so tenderly treated the historian does not
record. He probably mars all his previous kindness
by throwing the stick, devil and all, into lake or
river.

But the demons of South and East Africa are as
water to whisky when compared to those of the
West Coast, where their expulsion wholesale, at
stated intervals is a necessity of existence. So
potent are they for evil that the people of Dahomey,
who may in a few weeks thereafter expel them
wholesale, sacrifice sheep and goats to them before
sowing their crops.† If they neglected this precaution, so powerful are evil spirits, no corn would
ripen, even should every demon be expelled before
it comes into ear. Along the coast, where large
towns have to be purged, the ceremonies are both
elaborate and protracted. Rude wicker figures of
elephants, tigers, cows, and other animals are made,

* Krapf.   † Winterbotham.

and carefully covered over with cloth.   Of these, one is set up before every house door.*   Each family needs a figure, and the animals are selected from a supposed connection between them and the spirits of departed ancestors.   Old Tiger-face's son would naturally select the animal whose name his father bore when taking part in the great ceremony of expelling devils from the town and from his own fireside.   The figures are intended as receptacles or places of temporary retreat for the demons when the process of purgation begins.

At 3 A.M. a tempest of noise begins simultaneously in all parts of the town.   Drums beat, bugles bray, horns roar, bells tingle, whistles screech.   Everything which can be made to emit sound is brought into requisition and kept going till the owner is exhausted, or the instrument gives way, a frequent occurrence.   This pandemonium of noise continues till high noon.   At that hour floors are swept, dusty corners turned out, the ashes of the previous day's fires carefully collected, and everything where a demon could lurk removed and placed inside the wicker figure at the door.   The images are then carried in tumultuous procession to the river and tossed into the water with beat of drum.   The demons dare not return ; they are now beyond the boundaries of the town, and but for untoward accidents men might live in peace for an indefinite time.   But as ill-luck will have it, the next tribe may be expelling their own devils, and these, turned out of comfortable quarters, may enter the newly

* Waddell.

purged territory and finding it unoccupied, take up
their abode there till once more carried to the river
and so cast out. Illustrations of this might be
multiplied indefinitely, but what has been given
may be taken as characteristic of a particular phase
of thought.

Now this belongs to an early and very rude state
of society—to the time before man had differen-
tiated clearly between the natural and supernatural,
and when he still believed himself to have power
over the unseen world. The condition has continued
among peoples far removed from the flowing current
of civilisation, and who had not invented the art of
writing. It has survived through the hunting,
pastoral, and agricultural stages of progress among
rude peoples, and seems to persist wherever man is
unable to record his thoughts in symbols readily
understood by his fellows. But although this
peculiar belief in man's powers over the world of
spirits persists in barbarous countries, to use a
common expression, we should hardly be prepared
for its persistency in Christian times in Europe, and
among the most highly educated communities in
civilised lands. Few peoples have enjoyed greater
educational advantages, so far as the bulk of the
peasantry is concerned, than the Scotch, and still we
find among them, even at the present day, many
persons who believe in man's power to call the devil
at will. That such faith should be found universal
among savages is consistent with all we know of the
progress of human thought ; that Christian communities should continue, generation after generation,

through millenniums of years, to believe in the power
of their religious teachers on the one hand, and of
their wizards and witches on the other, to control
demons and influence nature, is one of those curious
phenomena which show how narrow are the limits
which divide savage man from civilised, and make us
pause to ask, how much of truth, absolute truth, we,
any of us, know concerning ourselves, and the
mysterious, unsatisfied yearnings of our souls for a
fuller, truer, and clearer knowledge of the unseen.

Not more than a century ago it was no uncommon
thing to appeal to priest or presbyter to visit this
village or that to " lay the devil," and the curious
thing is, that men of education and experience of the
world went through the mummeries supposed to
have that effect. A priest of the Braes of Lochaber
" laid " the devil about what is now Spean Bridge,
and the Reformed faith proceeded no farther up the
glen of the Spean. A successor of his, however,
doubted whether he had but half laid him in
Inveroy, the next district to Spean Bridge, the
inhabitants of which, according to the worthy father,
did justice neither to God nor man. This " laying "
of the devil was rendered necessary through his
being " raised " by persons who had that power
being in league with him, and without whose aid he
" could not leave his hole." How this was done I
have failed to discover with certainty. The " laying " was by bell, book and candle, or within Refor-
mation times " by prayer and the exercise of the
power of prayer," a phrase as difficult of interpreta-
tion as any African oracle of them all. Prayer one

can understand, but what is the " power of prayer " as applied to the " laying " of the devil? As to the " raising " of his majesty, one old man told me the following incident, for the truth of which he vouched on personal knowledge, " for," said he, " it happened when I was a good bit o' a callant." I give his own words as nearly as I can remember.

" It's a long time since, but I mind it as if it were yesterday. The boys were having a wild night. Two old men had just finished wi' a pickle malt for the new year like, and there was plenty going. About the middle of the night, at the turn as you would say, one of the young men began to curse and swear awful. He called on the devil, and said he might come and take him. Some o' them were a wee sober, and bade him keep quiet, but he gaed worse, and defied a' the devils in hell, and said he would like to smell their brimstone. That moment there was an awful flash of lightning, and a woman, said no to be canny, or the likes o' her, came down the chimney and stood afore him. She stood facing him, and said : ' Ye want to see the devil : he may be here sooner nor ye think.' Sorry a word more did she say when the house was filled wi' burning brimstone, and something going up and down in a blue flame on the crook"—[i.e., the chain for hanging pots over the fire]. " Then it made a noise such as the like was never heard, and gaed out o' sight. The gun-barrels in the house were twisted and broken, and the next day the smell o' brimstone was strong on their clothes. None of them could ever tell right how it happened, but there's nae doubt about it.

It's as true as gospel." And then the old man proceeded to detail other experiences of his youth, and to bemoan the scepticism of the age, which was sure to bring the curse of God down upon the world. This was not an ignorant man, but one fairly well informed; a man who knew his Bible, and could correct preachers on points of Calvinistic theology. I knew him well, and he represented current opinion among middle-aged and old people in parts of the Highlands about twenty years ago. How the devil was "laid" in this case my informant did not remember, but he was fully informed how it was done in other cases, and believed as firmly as he did in his own existence that the art "was known to many of the godly in olden times."

There is a woman of my acquaintance in Reay who can "do things." Some years ago she asked a coach-driver for a "sail" in his vehicle. He refused. "Very well," said Annie; "I will be in Thurso before you." A mile farther on one of his horses fell stone dead, and he had the mortification of seeing the witch pass with an air of triumph. The owner has never refused her a "sail" since then.

A former minister of the parish of Reay in Caithness, a Mr. Pope, was a man of more than local reputation. He came to the parish when the people were largely pagan, and being a man of herculean strength, used gentle physical persuasion by means of an oaken cudgel, known as the "bailiff," to bring his parishioners to church. His feats of strength, and especially his having first thrashed, and then driven before him to church, a local character regarded with dread as a giant in strength and a tiger in temper, gave him an extraordinary influence over his unruly flock. Supernatural powers were freely attributed to him, and this for reasons of his own he may have encouraged. Among other powers he possessed he was regarded as being able to "lay the devil" at will. It so happened that the people of Strathy, in the neighbouring parish, "raised" the fiend but could not get him "laid" again. In dire extremity they went to Mr. Pope, and on some pretext induced him to visit Strathy. When nearing the place "he got the smell of the fiend," and knew why they had sent for him. He was excessively angry, but having gone so far he proceeded to the place, and so effectually did he dispose of their troublesome visitor, that, as I was told last summer, "the devil has never since been raised in the district."

Did the scope of our inquiry permit, illustrations of the same practice of expelling the devil could be drawn from the usages of the Teutonic peoples of Europe. This is represented by such practices as are observed among the Finns of Eastern Russia. There on the last day of the year a band of young girls march through the streets and stop at each house corner, which they beat with wands they carry for the purpose. As they beat each house they say, in chorus, "We are driving Satan out of the village." After they have in this manner visited all the houses, they march in procession to the river, singing as they go, and when they arrive there throw their wands, devils and all, into the water to float away down stream. "At Brunnen, in Switzerland, the boys go about in procession on Twelfth Night, carrying torches and lanterns, and making a great noise with horns, cowbells, and whips. This is said to frighten away two female spirits of the wood—Strudeli and Strätteli."* These are but illustrations of the simpler forms of a custom observed by all the peoples of Europe; a custom which in many cases became grafted on to the services of the Christian Church,† no man can tell how, but which clearly carry us back to an age when the peoples of Europe were, by painful experience, groping their way towards a knowledge of truth, as the Central African of to-day is undoubtedly doing. For what are all religions but a searching after truth; the expression of man's desire to attain to a true and final knowledge of causes, and his own relation to these?

* Usener, quoted by J. G. Frazer.

† In Ross-shire there is a common custom when drinking from a road-side spring to tie a bit of rag to a branch or tuft of grass. This I have heard explained as an offering to the spirit of the spring, while others say it is to ban evil from the water. In either case it is a survival of a long-forgotten past—a simple action, carrying us back to a time when spirits inhabited every grove and running stream.

CHAPTER VII

WITCHCRAFT

WHEN man reached the conception of good and evil spirits as personal and separate existences—that is to say, beings capable of being influenced by him and having an influence over him—it needed but the advent of a Milton to set the gods by the ears. But before the Miltonic conception was reached there was a long transition period during which the gods set men by the ears. We have seen that kings and divine priests claimed to have in their own persons: first, the spirit of the creative and reproductive powers of nature ; next, that of their ancestors and predecessors, this latter passing over to the idea of an impersonal god. These were the beneficent patrons of men, who gave them rain, sunshine, crops, fecundity, successful hunting, and kindred blessings. During the world's youth the want of these was attributed to the negligence of the king, and with the lapse of time, perhaps to his malice or ill-will, as when the king was said " to have a bad heart." It was no uncommon experience for the king to be called sharply to task when the course of nature got into confusion and disorder, and men began to feel the pinch of want or the inconvenience of having to travel far afield for game. With the

advent of evil spirits the blame could be laid on
their shoulders for all the ills that afflicted humanity.
Evil persons were supposed to be in league with
those evil spirits, and to be their agents in carrying
out their nefarious purposes. As the good spirits
acted for men's benefit through the king or tribal
priest, so other malign spirits acted through persons
whose whole object was pure mischief for its own
sake, except when bribed to do good actions by
large gifts. The expulsion of spirits had not yet
occurred to man; propitiation did not always suit
his purpose; and yet the case required that drastic
remedies should be adopted. It was obviously a
matter of the first importance that means should be
discovered for the detection and extermination, if
possible, of the class of persons who brought the ills
from which men suffered upon them.

In earlier times the king himself was frequently
put to death when he failed to order the course of
nature regularly, and give the blessings expected
from him, and if so, there could be no hesitation or
doubt about the art of those who wilfully disturbed
the course of nature being a capital crime, or rather
the capital crime beyond all others even by comparison. For to savage man there is no crime com-
parable to witchcraft in malignity of purpose and
object. Here, then, we have the origin of that system
of jurisprudence and religious ritual which, projecting itself into civilised and Christian times, pursued
its victims, under the sanction of civil law and
church judicatories, as persons who ought not to
live. Primitive faith, or superstition as we call it

now, clung for generations to men professing to be disciples of Him who came to show the higher and better way, so tenaciously that they could, without pity or compunction, see their fellows amidst blazing faggots for an imaginary crime. If the growth of thought has been so slow within historic times, and among a people with a written language, what must it have been among primitive men ? When religion, with all the sanction it received from the sacred books of Christianity, took so many centuries to realise such elementary facts regarding man's relation to the supernatural, do we wonder that millenniums pass without any appreciable difference in custom and myth among savages ?

But how were wizards and witches to be discovered when the world was young, and before men learned to recognise the " witch's mark ? " Spirits bent on evil gave no outward token of their presence so far as that could possible be avoided. These spirits would only be harboured by persons of the most malignant disposition, or who for some reason had a grudge against their kind. So the spirits sought out those who, through neglect or illtreatment, had been soured and rendered bitter in heart against their fellows.* Thus it happened that deformed persons, and those who through any infirmity were unable to take their place and act their part in life like their fellows, were believed to be possessed of the devil, or, in other words, were wizards and witches. Dwarfs, dumb persons, women who never were sought in marriage, and those with

* J. Sutton, MS. notes.

any facial peculiarities or defects which made them conspicuous, were most frequently regarded as the incarnation of the evil spirit of the world. From them it was impossible to expel or allure the demon as in the case of a patient who was devil-possessed, for, unlike the sick, the devil dwelt within the wizards by their own will and choice. They were themselves devils incarnate as the king or high priest was incarnate god. Such being the case, the only hope of safety, the sole means of security, lay in the rigid enforcement of that curious Mosaic enactment: "Thou shall not suffer a witch to live."*

Let us now consider how man, as he groped his way towards a higher conception of truth and the facts with which he found himself surrounded in the world, sought to protect himself against the malign influences exercised by those persons who entered into league with evil spirits, for the purpose of injuring their kind. And here it will be better to begin with the southern portion of Africa, with the customs of which I am familiar, and which have been studied and recorded with a greater degree of minuteness than those of any other part of the continent. In any study of witchcraft it must be borne in mind that the wizard's power is unlimited, or only bounded by such limitations and restrictions as the gods are subject to. Evil spirits are as powerful as good; hence it follows that the good must have assistance from man himself, if they are to cope successfully with evil. Man and the gods

* Exod. xxii. 18.

may keep evil in check. Either of them alone would be unequal to the task. Can the beneficent god give rain? The wizard can thwart his purpose by the simplest of expedients. Can he make domestic animals prolific? The wizard has but to get a hair out of a cow's tail to bring murrain among them. Does the "father of men" give easy delivery to mothers? The wizard causes death in childbed or blights the offspring with a curse. Throughout the whole circle of social and domestic life the good designs of Providence and the gods can be frustrated by the art of witchcraft, and, indeed, the wizard may in a sense, be said to be more powerful than the gods. To them belong the initiative; all things are under their control and ordered by them; and the wizard has but to lie in wait till the gods act, and then, by the practice of his art, frustrates their intentions by marring their work. He, on the other hand, is safe from assault by the gods, for he never initiates any original work on his own account. His business is to watch their doings, and when they favour men to bring calamity and death.

So the Hottentot priest, when he sacrifices for any purpose, takes the most extraordinary precautions against malign influences. He keeps his purpose a profound secret, lest his intentions should become known to some "suspect person." At the sacrifice none must be present except such as can be fully trusted. And here lies his chief difficulty. Wizards are as cunning as are evil spirits themselves, and adopt every kind of disguise so as to remain unsuspected. He can guard against the presence of reputed wizards and suspect persons. But these have "friends" who are neither known nor suspected, and should one of them be present to inform the wizard of what goes on, and convey to him as much as a single hair from the sacrifice, or even a blade of grass from the spot on which an important person, as the chief or priest, sat, he can accomplish all the evil that he could have done by his presence among the crowd. For some reason, which I never could discover, suspect persons cannot be, or at all events are not, put on trial till specific acts can be charged against them before a properly constituted tribunal. They cannot even be shut up by such methods as we have often found so convenient beyond St. George's Channel.

Under such circumstances it is necessary to have a method by which guilt can be easily and surely brought home to those practising the unlawful art. This is done by a class of men known as witch-doctors. These are really magicians or priests, who, because of the dignity of their calling, occupy a premier position among the religious teachers of Africa. They are permitted to have armed retainers, and to rank on an equality with heads of clans. Their places of residence are sanctuaries; they hold court and try causes; their persons are sacred, and in virtue of their office they are entitled to receive fees in connection with all cases and trials. The following may be taken as illustrative of the witch-doctor's method of procedure :—When any one, say a man in middle life, falls ill, his friends, believing him to be bewitched, repair to the witch-doctor's house, and sit down outside in a waiting attitude. After a brief interval the doctor appears, says " Good morning," and then sitting down, takes a leisurely pinch of snuff. If the visitors ask for tobacco, he knows it is but an ordinary call, and enters into conversation on current topics. If they do not ask a pinch, he retires to his house, and returns with a dry hide and a small bundle of sticks which he throws down before his visitors. He then says, " You have come about a child ? "

They, beating softly on the hide, reply : " We agree."

The doctor proceeds : " You are going to speak about a woman ? "

" We agree," say the strangers, while they continue their gentle beating.

" The man you have come about is very ill," may be the doctor's next remark.

" We agree, we agree," cry out the visitors, this time beating violently.

On such lines the doctor proceeds till he has learned all he wishes to know : the man's age ; whether of a strong or weakly constitution ; how long he has been ill ; whether he has any known enemy, and his means. After this he sits a long while in silence, and then says, oracularly, " You are being killed." When asked how and by whom, he replies that he cannot tell ; they must return on the following day, and meantime the gods may divulge to him the secret. He mentions his fee, generally an ox, as a. retainer, and this must be brought when they return next day, otherwise no revelations will be made to him. He is the servant of the gods, and what is given to him is offered to them. The deputation then retire, and when they go home a trusted friend receives a hint as to whom they suspect of bewitching the patient. This neighbour goes at dead of night, and has an interview with the doctor, who is now in a position to act. A muster of villagers is duly called, attendance at which is compulsory on pain of confessed guilt. The accused marches, in ignorance of his doom, with the cavalcade On the way he may be casually asked, "What does the person bewitching our brother deserve?" and he of course promptly replies, "He must die."

The ritual followed at the meeting varies, but the following is one method. All the villagers give up their arms to the doctor's guard, and then seat themselves in a semicircle. The doctor sings, dances, capers and mutters incantations within the circle of expectant sitters; then rushing up to the doomed man cries out, "This is the wizard who bewitched so and so, the gods name him." He then runs in among his armed guards, and all the people jump up, leaving the culprit sitting alone. He must not move, nor will any one go near him. No one is allowed to plead his cause even if they wished. His friends are disarmed and cannot strike a blow for him. The man's doom is inexorably fixed, and his only chance of escape is the somewhat slender one of the chief ordering an ox to be substituted and offered as a sacrifice; this, or a clean pair of heels, if he can show them. On crossing the border of the tribal territory he is safe, there being no extradition treaty for wizards.

As we move northwards we find the same or even greater precautions taken against witchcraft, but the system of jurisprudence is modified. . In the Nyassa region, for example, the office of discovering persons who practise the illegal art falls not to the priest, but to the prophetess, who is frequently the principal wife of the chief, and one of the most formidable and justly dreaded persons met with in Africa. It is to the prophetess the ancestral spirits make known the will of the gods. When she sees these face to face, which always happens at the dead hour of night, she begins by raving and screaming, which she continues till the whole village is astir, and she herself utterly prostrated by her exertions ; she then throws herself on the ground in a kind of trance, during which the villagers gather round her, awe-stricken, waiting for the oracle of the god, for she is now god-possessed. After such possession and revelations she may impose impossible tasks on men, and these they will attempt without question as their destiny.* She may demand human sacrifices, and no one dare deny her victims. Suppose she declares a victim must be offered to a mountain deity—for there are gods of the valleys and gods of the hills, deities of the river and of the forest —the victim is conducted to the spot indicated and bound hand and foot to a tree, If during the first night he is killed by beasts of prey, the gods have accepted the sacrifice ; if not, he is left to die of

* Rev. Duff Macdonald.

starvation or thrown into a pool. The slave was not worthy the god's acceptance ; he is of no further use to any one.

It is, however, as a detective of wizards and witches the prophetess is in most constant demand. When she travels on such duty she is accompanied by a strong guard ; and when she orders a meeting of a clan or tribe attendance is compulsory. When all are assembled, our friend, who is clad with a scanty loin cloth and literally covered from head to heels with rattles and fantasies, rushes about among the crowd in the most frantic manner. She shouts and raves and rants like one demented. After which, assuming a calm judicial manner, she goes from one to another touching each person's hand. As she touches the hand of the bewitcher, she starts back with a loud shriek and yells, " This is him, the murderer. Blood is in his hand."* Having discovered the culprit, she next proceeds to prove his guilt. This she does by " finding the horns " he used in the prosecution of the unlawful art. These are generally the horns of a small species of antelope which are *par excellence* " witches' horns." She finds the horns by going along the bank of the stream from which the family of the bewitched person got water. At intervals she lifts water from the stream, which she pours upon the ground, and then stoops to listen. Spirit voices direct her to the wizard's hiding-place. Arrived there, she begins to dig with a hoe she carries, muttering incantations as she works, and there she finds the incriminating horns. †

* Rev. Duff Macdonald.   † *Ibid.*

Now, how does the prophetess find the horns?
By what devil's art does she hit upon the spot
where they are concealed? The explanation is to
us very simple, but the African has not yet
discovered it, or if he has, no one has dared
to say so. Wherever she is employed she must
spend a night at the village before she begins
operations. She does not retire to rest with the
other villagers, but wanders about the live-long
night listening to spirit voices. If she sees a villager
outside his door after the usual hour for retiring, she
brings that up against him next day as evidence
of guilty intention, and that, either on his own
account or the wizard's, he meant to steal away
to dig up the horns. The fear of such consequences
keeps all persons within doors, and leaves the
prophetess free to arrange for the tableau of the
next day. So far is the fear of witchcraft carried,
that whole villages have been known to partake of
the ordeal poison in order to root out evil persons.*
If a man is guilty, he dies; if not guilty, even if
caught in the act red-handed, he recovers—he was in
that case not a thief, he was bewitched to make him
steal. Such is the Wayao philosophy of trial by
ordeal.

Among the Bongo on the White Nile no communication can be had with the spirit world except by
means of certain roots which are known to the
magicians.† These are of service, not only in holding communication with the gods, but in warding
off all evil influences. Had the secret been kept, the

* Rev. Duff Macdonald.　　　　　† Schweinfurth.

Bongo would have been the happiest people under the sun, but in an evil hour some noted wizard discovered it and made the world unhappy. With this knowledge in their possession, old people may apparently be lying peaceably in their beds while their spirits range the forest by moonlight in search of the magic roots.* These spirits assume animal form, which remind us of the familiar stories of farmers wounding hares, and hearing of old women in the next village having broken arm or leg mysteriously, which they set and dressed without aid of doctor; assured sign that the fear of his seeing the bullet-mark prevented their seeking his aid.

The Bongo priest who has obtained the coveted roots, can only hold communication with the gods in the approved manner by falling into a trance and receiving their commands in dreams and visions. The wizard, wielding equally potent spells, and restricted by no canons of custom, can leave the visible body, as the soul does in sleep, his only risk being the body being stolen during the spirit's absence, enter a hyæna, and range over mountain and plain, working evil as he goes. When a people are exposed to such dangers, to exorcise ghosts, demons, wood goblins, and all evil spirits and persons, must ever be their chief religious duty. When the destiny of a nation depends on guarding against evil influences of a spiritual nature, that people must be regarded as deeply religious, however little their rites may attract the attention of those who visit them.

* Schweinfurth.

Dr. Schweinfurth, who is one of our best authorities on the usages of tribes living on the upper reaches of the Nile, says that some of them have hardly any religion. The Niam-niam, he says, have no religion, and use for divinity the word for lightning.* It is curious so observant a traveller should have been so far misled as to what constitutes religious observances. We are familiar in Zululand, Nyassa region, and in Uganda with the use of the term for lightning—in each case a different word— for heaven, thunder, or the god, and these peoples are among the most religious communities in Africa. When a man cannot knock his foot against a tree stump without attaching to it a supernatural significance† that man is religious whether he has a separate word for his god or not. The statement seems all the more inexplicable when we find the doctor himself saying that the same Niam-niam, who have no religion, " have a word for prayer "; that they practise augury, and believe in goblins, ghosts, and witches, the latter of which are treated by them as they have always been by persons with properly constituted minds—that is, by getting rid of them in the manner most approved for the extermination of the pestilent race. If the Niam-niam have no religion, to whom do they pray ? Whence came their goblins ? How do their witches attain their power except by spirit agency ? These are questions which must be satisfactorily disposed of before we can accept a general statement that a people have

* Schweinfurth.
† Rev. Duff Macdonald; Dr. Elmslie, MS. notes.

been found who have no religion—that is, no faith in regard to supernatural powers or agents.

If the Nile tribes conduct their witch prosecutions, and religious services generally, in so perfunctory a manner as to attract the attention of travellers but slightly, their deficiency is more than made up by the Bullom tribes of the West Coast. When they drink beer they pour out a few drops as a religious act ; when they eat, particles of food are allowed to fall on the ground for the same purpose.* They can neither walk nor sit, sow nor reap, hunt nor fish, without performing acts of devotion and dutiful obedience to the gods. They move among divinities, and these may be disturbed by loud laughter, by improper movements, or by words which can imply disparagement of the gods or their works. Each day has its own religious duties, but it is in the " witch palaver " their true devotion and fidelity to the will of the gods is seen to best advantage.

Their three great palavers are, " sauce palaver," " woman palaver," and " witch palaver." † In the first, which refers to all ordinary offences, the case is conducted according to the ordinary rules of evidence, either by witnesses or the ordeal. The accused is held as guilty, and he must prove his innocence. If he have witnesses, good ; if not, then the poison bowl. The same remarks apply to " woman palaver," only that in this case the accused must submit to the ordeal. What that ordeal is we

* Walker.   † Winterbotham.

shall see in another connection ; our present business
is with the " witch palaver." In this case the
accused can prove his innocence by no other means
than the ordeal. When the offence was committed
he may have been on a journey, at sea, asleep, sick
and unable to move, on the war path ; in any condition or circumstances. None of these things can
be admitted in evidence nor in mitigation of sentence.
Persons who have the power of transforming themselves into animals or insects, feigning sleep, or even
death, so perfectly as to deceive the very elect—that
is to say, the authoritative religious guides of the
community—are not to be trifled with. So it is,
when a suspect is on trial for specific acts of witchcraft, a red hot-iron is applied to his skin, partly to
jog his memory, but principally that the brand may
be examined to determine how much skin adheres
to the hot metal, whether the wound bleeds, and
how its edges " curl."* To each of these signs great
importance is attached in determining presumption
of guilt. This ordeal may be final and satisfactory,
but the probabilities are against it. The show is
too good to be over so soon, and the red-hot poker
is succeeded by a jar of oil, which is placed on the
fire till it boils. Into this boiling oil a stone, made
red hot in the fire, is now dropped and the culprit
directed to fish it out with his naked hand.†
According to the condition of the hand after the
ordeal is the presumption of guilt or innocence. If

* Winterbotham.
† *Ibid.*; Rev. Duff Macdonald.

these means do not conclusively prove the case, he must drink " red water." * This is a decoction which is prepared by the priest in public from poisonous substances. After the preparation is made the priest washes his hands, as well as the mortar and pestle used, as a ceremonial act. The accused for a similar reason must rinse his mouth with clean water. He is then given a quantity of boiled rice which he must eat; after it he drinks the poison. If the red water acts as an emetic, and that vomiting continues till he brings up particles of rice, he is innocent and escapes; the red water ran away from him. When it does not act as an emetic, even if the man does not die from the effects of the poison, he is guilty; the red water clung to him. Sometimes the drug causes purging. In this case the culprit has " spoiled the red water"; the augury is doubtful, and to remove all difficulties he is sold—out of the territory, it is needless to say.

This latter form of ordeal is common in cases of supposed adultery among many tribes of the West Coast, as well as throughout the whole of the Lake region of Central Africa, and is specially worthy of note because of its close resemblance to, if not identity with, the practice of trial by ordeal for the same offence among the Jews : " If a man's wife go aside, and commit a trespass against him, and a man lie with her carnally, and it be hid from the eyes of her husband, and be kept close . . . . And the spirit of jealousy come upon him, and he be jealous of his wife, and she be defiled ; or, if the spirit of

---

* Winterbotham.

jealousy come upon him, and he be jealous of his
wife, and she be not defiled, then shall the man bring
his wife unto the priest . . . . And the priest shall
take holy water in an earthen vessel ; . . . . And
the priest shall have in his hand the bitter water
that causeth the curse . . . . And the priest shall
write three curses in a book, and he shall blot them
out with the bitter water, and he shall cause the
woman to drink the bitter water that causeth the
curse . . . . And when he hath made her to drink the
water, then it shall come to pass, if she be defiled,
and have done trespass against her husband, that
the water that causeth the curse shall enter into her
and become bitter, and her belly shall swell, and her
thigh shall rot, and the woman shall be a curse
among her people.   And if the woman be not defiled
but be clean, then she shall be free."*   The connection between this enactment in the Mosaic legislation and the practice among primitive men, it is not
my province to trace in the present essay, but the
resemblance is so striking that the inference seems
plain enough.

Turning to the history of witchcraft among
civilised peoples, we have in it perhaps the best
illustration of the persistency in popular imagination of the belief in the supreme power of evil
spirits, and in man's power to influence the course of
nature by necromancy and magic.   It would be easy
to cite examples from every country in Europe to
show how the same belief in the power of evil,
personified in wizards and witches, influenced the

* Numbers. v. 12-28.

whole domestic and social life of the people. In Jut-
land a rowan growing out of the top of another tree
is exceedingly efficacious against witchcraft.* This
tree has the same virtue in Scotland, and I knew a
worthy farmer's wife, who died only a few years ago,
and who annually, in early summer, had a St.
Andrew's cross made of rowan twigs, which she
placed in the cowhouse as a talisman against the
arts of witches. German farmers use the mistletoe
for a similar purpose. In the island of Rum it was
believed that if one of the family of Lachlin—a local
family of note—shot a deer on the mountain of
Finchra, he would either die on the spot or contract
a distemper from which he could not recover.†
This may belong to the class of totems rather than
to witchcraft. Traces of clan totems are frequently
met with in the north and west of Scotland.

Confining ourselves to this country, we have ample
evidence, in the witch and fairy cult still current,
of the ancient belief in man's power to influence
nature and the lives of his fellow-men. And not the
least curious thing is, that the persons accused of
witchcraft often claimed to possess the power
ascribed to them, though this meant an alternative
between faggots and a deep pool. Among savage
men, on the contrary, denial is all but universal
when one is accused of having communication with
evil spirits, or exercising the art of witchcraft.
Among Scottish witches and fairy folk we get
glimpses of persons of different grades, some of them
holding high office and directing the affairs of the

* Kamp.   † Martin.

peculiar community to which they belong. Thus, in the confessions of Isabella Gowdie, indicted for witch-craft at Nairn in 1662, we have a King and Queen of Fairyland. "I was," said Isabella when in the dock, "in Downie hill, and got meat from the Queen of the Fairies, and more that I could eat. The queen is brawly clothed in white linen and in white and brown cloth; and the king is a braw man, well-favoured and broad-faced. There were plenty of elf bulls, rowting and skoyling up and down, and affrighted me."* Mr. Kirk, from whom I quote, adds, that on the authority of local tradition, fairy-land is well supplied with musical instruments and books of history, travel, plays, novels, biography, but no Bibles—the lack of the latter owing to the fairy folk being in league with the devil, from whom they receive their government and power.

Before our familiar fairy cult was evolved, the evil spirits of primitive man had crystallised into a personal devil, supreme and all-powerful, with numerous attendant angels or messengers, and it is curious to note that something very nearly akin to this is met with in Ashantee, where the king has a thousand "Kra," or souls.‡ The Kra are the king's spies, a kind of secret service guild, and are called the king's souls, because when he dies they are all put to death that they may attend upon him in the land of shades. To strike, or even touch a Kra, is not only a deadly insult, but a serious capital crime. It is doing it to the king himself; and it is quite consistent with savage thought to regard a powerful king and his

* Kirk.   † Kühne and Rameyer.

Kra as still actively engaged in connection with the
world's affairs long after they have quitted the upper
air.   He is chief dictator, and each of his souls do
his behests in the affairs of men.   This is the
common doctrine of witchcraft as that lives in
popular imagination.   The black art is something
carried on under the direction of a supreme evil
spirit, who is assisted by a countless host of minor
devils or angels ; that is to say, messengers, Kra, or
souls. · This doctrine must have been developed
when man reached the conception of a supreme
spirit of good, opposed by a supreme spirit of
evil.   But in tracing the growth of the idea of
one supreme spirit of good, or god, we are met by
greater difficulties than in tracing the doctrine of
devils, for the latter took shape and colour from the
former.   When man found a supreme spirit among
the gods, he had to account for the fact that he did
not, or could not, at all times order events for the good
of man.   Evil still persisted ; so he concluded there
must be a supreme and personal devil, who commanded such agencies in the unseen world as were
at the disposal of the good god himself.

The difficulty of tracing the growth of the idea of
a supreme god arises from the impossibility of determining with certainty what was originally a local
or tribal deity, and what a spirit regarded
generally as supreme.   We have seen that the Zulu
term Mlungu, and its equivalents may mean, great
ancestor, lightning, the powers of nature generally,
or god, and we have at least one instance which
seems to show how such ideas as that of Mlungu first

take hold of the popular imagination, and become
almost universal myth, for myth it is when all has
been said, but myth which describes a sober fact of
human faith and the progress of thought. The Rev.
Duff Macdonald, a careful observer, who lived several
years in Central Africa, says of the Wayao, that
they not only worship their own ancestors, as is
common to most Africans, but also invoke by prayer
and sacrifice the gods of the country who were
worshipped by the people they expelled. The older
inhabitants were compelled to retire before the
advance of the Wayao, but their great god Kangomba remained undisturbed on Mount Socki, nor
would he be displaced by the newer divinities
or the arts of magic.* So it is that the present
chief, Kapeni, when making annual supplication and
sacrifice, asks some noted Wanyasa priest to
come to his assistance. The Wanyasa are related
to the people whose god Kangomba originally was,
and their presence is acceptable to him. Such a god
as this, though originally a local tribal deity—some
remote ancestor of a chief—gradually gathers more
than a local reputation. The Wanyasa priests
officiating at his annual festivals will carry his fame
to their own people, and bring the Wanyasa tribe,
through association with the Wayao at his festivals,
to worship him in times of stress and trial at
their own homes. If he grants their prayer his
reputation will speedily spread as both powerful and
good. Besides, every African who returns from a
journey exaggerates all his experiences, and adorns

* Rev. Duff Macdonald.

his narratives with gorgeous imagery.   In this way
Kangomba will lose nothing of his glory and power
by distance. He will be spoken of in every Wanyasa
village as great beyond all local deities, and may,
in a few generations, occupy a place second only to
Mlungu himself.

Such probably was the origin of Mlungu when
first men worshipped him, and if so, it furnishes us
with the key we have been striving to find as to how
primitive men arrived at the idea of a supreme god,
and from that deduced the doctrine of a supreme
devil, on which he hangs all the traditions he has
regarding witchcraft and kindred evils.   It will also
help us to understand much with which we have
long been familiar, though we may not have understood the relation of facts to one another.   Such
conceptions of deity and of evil are consistent with
the acknowledgment of Nebuchadnezzar, that the
God of Daniel was supreme among the gods—greater
than those of the mighty empire itself.

We have now arrived at an advanced period of
the world's progress in thought.   If the theory
suggested is correct, the African, starting with the
crude idea that men could influence the course of
nature, and that the power to do so was vested in
his king, who was god—the personification of nature
herself—advanced a long way when he conceived
his chief, whose body he had buried or burned, still
living and taking an active interest in the world's
affairs.   As thought progressed and man began to
differentiate more accurately, he reached the doctrine
of all human souls living in a land of spirits, thus

making his way towards the conception of immortality, and that instead of the world's forces being regulated by caprice, there were good and evil spirits at work. To secure success to the good, good men sought for means of thwarting the evil. The evil, on the other hand, not to be baulked of their object, sought out agents on whom they conferred supernatural powers. This war of good and evil could not long continue before certain of the good spirits, or evil, attained to a place of supreme power. In tracing the history of witchcraft and the methods adopted to eradicate its votaries, we find how naturally man came to believe in persons possessing supernatural powers for evil. We have also seen, casually, the growth and development of another order, magicians and prophets; but before endeavouring to trace the history of prophecy among primitive peoples, it may be best to consider some of their festivals, as those of first-fruits and harvest, where magicians or prophets are seen to best advantage in the exercise of their functions ; after which we can the better understand the development of the order and the importance attached to the office.

CHAPTER VIII

HARVEST FESTIVALS

THE festivals and ceremonial acts of any people give a clue to the original form of their institutions, and when these can be compared with what still exists, in its original form, among untutored nations, it affords evidence which is of the first importance in tracing the development of religion and the growth of civilisation.

The Yam festivals, as observed in Ashantee, were referred to in considering substitutionary sacrifice, and we saw how closely bound up with the religious life of the people are all the facts relating to the ripening of crops and the gathering in of the harvest. Nor is this peculiar to Ashantee. Everywhere the feasts of first-fruits are intimately associated with the religious observances of the people and the homage which they render to the gods. Among savages this homage is to the powers of nature, whose efforts are crowned with success when the creative and reproductive spirit of vegetation yields its increase to man. When a Pondo chief is to hold the feast of first-fruits, some of his people procure a ripe plant of the gourd family, pumpkin or calabash, from another tribe. This is cooked; the inside cleaned out, and the rind made ready for use as a vessel. It is then presented to the chief with much ceremony.* The first-fruits are now brought forward, and a sacrifice, generally a young bull, is offered, after which the feast commences. The chief issues certain orders for the conduct of the proceedings, tastes the fruits which are served in the gourd dish with which he has been presented, and then abdicates all his functions while the festival lasts.

The cattle from all the neighbouring villages are collected in the vicinity, and now they are brought together, and the bulls incited to fight to determine which is to be king among them for the next year. The young people engage in games and dances, feats of strength and running. After these are over the whole community give themselves over to disorder, debauchery, and riot. In their bull-fights and games they but did honour to the powers of nature, and now, as they eat and drink, the same powers are honoured in another form and by other rites. There is no one in authority to keep order, and every man does what seems good in his own eyes. Should a man stab his neighbour he escapes all punishment, and so too with all other crimes against the person, property, and morality. People are even permitted to abuse the chief to his face, an offence which at any other time would meet with summary vengeance and an unceremonious dispatch to join the ancestors. While the feast continues a deafening noise is kept up by drumming, shouting, hand-clapping, and every kind of instrument that can be made to emit sound. Men advance to the chief and explain their origin,

* J. Sutton, MS. notes.

and also the object they hold sacred, by imitating the sounds and movements of their most sacred animal. This is the person's totem. Others imitate the gurgling made by an enemy when stabbed in the throat. Those who adopt this latter emblem are known as " children of the spear."

When the ceremonies, revels, and mummeries are ended, the chief repairs to his accustomed place, and sitting down there, by that act resumes his kingly functions. He calls the bravest of his braves before him, who is immediately clothed and decorated with skins of animals suggestive of courage and strategy. He performs a dance amid the frenzied shouting of the multitude, after which the chief declares the festival at an end and harvest commenced.*

The facts deserving of special notice here are the sacrifice, the fighting of the bulls, and the honour done to the reproductive powers of nature. These, and the abdication of the chief, would lead to the inference that the festival is a true survival of what, in earlier times and under a ruder system, existed when a temporary king was appointed and killed as a sacrifice, the incarnate god himself being slain that nature might revive in spring. Whether from such facts men came at last to infer a resurrection of the body, it is impossible to determine. The Pondos are not singular in their observance of harvest customs. The Hos of North-east India have a notion that at this period men and women are so overcharged with vicious propensities that it is absolutely necessary to let off steam by allowing

* J. Sutton, MS. notes.

for a time full vent to their passions.* For the time they give themselves up to feasting, drinking, and debauchery. The men lose all respect for the women and for themselves, and the women all notions of modesty. Usually the Hos are a quiet, reserved, and well-behaved moral people, but at the harvest festival all this is reversed, and their nature seems to undergo a complete change. The curious thing is, that when all is over they settle down into their old steady, sober habits as if nothing had happened.

But what is most peculiar about harvest festivals and feasts of first-fruits is, their close resemblance to one another among all peoples the world over, and how near those of civilised man are to the savage ; differing not in kind, but only in the manner of conducting them ; thus showing to us, that they are among the most ancient and primitive of man's ritual and customs. For example. The Peruvians believe that all useful plants are animated by a divine being, that is spirit, who causes their growth.† These divine beings are named after the particular plant, as the Maize mother, the Rice mother, or the Potato mother. Figures of these mothers made from the stalks of the respective plants, and dressed in women's clothes, are worshipped. As the mother, these figures had power of giving birth to or producing much rice, maize, or potatoes, as the case might be,‡ and in this acted according as they were treated. The Peruvian mother of the Maize was kept a whole year, and burned at the time of harvest :

---

* Dalton, "Ethnology of Bengal," quoted by J. G. Frazer.
† J. G. Frazer.   ‡ Mannhardt.

when a fresh one took her place. During the
festival, eating drinking and general rejoicing goes
on.   In Ashantee all laws are abrogated for one
day at the Yam festival, and for the time every man
does whatever he pleases.   One custom observed is
to bring out, to be placed before the fetish house,
the skulls of noted enemies killed in war, and it is
said the skull of an English baronet did duty for
many years—in fact, was still in existence, kept in a
brass basin, when the late king's power was over-
thrown by the English.   The people during the day
of liberty give themselves up to dancing and revelry.
Executioners caper about, ornamented with necklets
made from the jaws of victims they slew as offerings or king's "messengers" to the nether world,
and with girdles of skulls.   Before eating the new
yams the king bathes in fetish water as a ceremonial
act ; when all is over he resumes his authority as
we saw done by the chief of Pondoland.

These customs, of which examples might be
multiplied from every region of Africa and the
heathen world generally, differ in no essential
feature, and are singularly like the survivals we have
in Europe.   In Aberdeenshire, Scotland, the last
sheaf cut, or " maiden," is carried home in merry procession by the harvesters.   It is then presented to
the mistress of the house, who dresses it up to be
preserved till the first mare foals.   The maiden is
then taken down and presented to the mare as its
first food.*   The neglect of this would have untoward
effects upon the foal, and disastrous consequences

* Miss J. Ligertwood, MS. notes.

upon farm operations generally for the season. In Caithness the person who cuts the last sheaf is called "winter," and so remains till next harvest. The sheaf itself is carefully preserved till it is displaced by another the following year. The Celts of the west country attached great importance to cutting the last sheaf. All the harvesters stood round in a circle while the youngest girl among the reapers cut a few straws left standing at the corner of the field for that purpose. This sheaf was ultimately used, as I have been assured by old people, for making Brüd's bed, which was as follows :—On Candlemas day the mistress and servants of each family take a sheaf of oats, and dress it up in women's apparel. They put it in a large basket, and beside it a club of wood. They then cry three times in chorus, " Brüd is come, Brüd is welcome." This is done just before they retire to rest, and in the morning they examine the ashes ; expecting to find among them the mark of Brüd's club. If they do, it is an indication of a prosperous year and good crops ; if not, the opposite.*

In the district of Lochaber, where dancing and merry-making on the last night of harvest used to be universal, and is still generally observed, the ceremonies without the "maiden" would be like a wedding without the bride. The maiden is carried home with tumultuous rejoicing, and after being suitably decorated is hung up in the barn, where the dancing usually takes place. After supper, which is served in the barn ball-room, and before

* Martin.

dancing begins, one of the company, generally the
oldest man present, fills himself a glass of whisky,
which he drinks, after he has turned his face to the
suspended sheaf and said : " Here's to the maiden."
The company follow his example, each in turn drinking to the " maiden." This I have seen done more
than once. Shall I add that I have myself done it ?
Very similar to this is the custom observed in
the neighbourhood of Dantiz, as recorded by Frazer,
who follows Mannhardt. He says : " When the
winter corn is cut and mostly bound up in sheaves,
the portion which still remains to be bound is divided
amongst the women binders, each of whom receives
a swath of equal length to bind. A crowd of
reapers, children, and idlers gathers round to witness
the contest, and at the word ' Seize the old man,'
the women fall to work, all binding their allotted
swaths as hard as they can. The spectators watch
them narrowly, and the woman who cannot keep
pace with the rest, and consequently binds the last
sheaf, has to carry the ' old man' (the last sheaf)
to the farm-house and deliver it to the farmer with
the words : ' Here I bring you the old man.' At
the supper which follows the ' old man' is placed
at the table and receives an abundant portion of
food, which, as he cannot eat it, falls to the share of
the woman who carried him. Afterwards the ' old
man' is placed in the yard, and all the people dance
round him. Further, the woman who bound the
last sheaf goes herself by the name of the ' old man'
till the next harvest ; and is often mocked with the
cry, ' Here comes the old man.' "

In Bavaria each reaper, as they are about to finish, has a patch to cut. They reap as fast as they can, and he who has to cut the last few handfuls " drives out the old man." Near Stettin the woman who binds the last sheaf has " the old man," and bears the nickname for a year. Formerly she was herself dressed up in pease-straw and carried home, when the harvesters danced with her till the straw fell off.

These examples illustrate the contests in reaping and binding, as well as the subsequent treatment of the sheaf and the person cutting it ; and when it is remembered that the person who is last at reaping represents the corn spirit, the idea is fully expressed by dressing him in corn straw. That it is the corn spirit that is represented is clearly seen from the customs of parts of Germany, where a man and woman, called the " oats' wife " and the " oats' man " dance at the harvest festival, after which the corn stalks are plucked from their bodies till not a particle is left. In these cases the idea is that the corn spirit—the " old man "—the woman, or maiden, is the last sheaf, and that the spirit lives in the barn during the winter. At sowing time it goes out to the fields again to resume its functions And, as we saw, in the giving of the maiden to the first mare that foals, in Aberdeenshire, and as is done in parts of the West Highlands, where it is distributed among the cows at Christmas, these functions include reproduction among cattle as well as growth of corn.

This points to our harvest customs as being a

survival from primitive times, and that in one form
or another they have passed down from generation
to generation, adapting themselves to all conditions
of life and of faith.   They carry us back to the wild
revelry that surrounded the man-god when he gave
his people the gifts of harvest.   They still have an
echo—faint it may be but real—of the days when the
chief abdicated for a time that he and his people
might do homage to the corn spirit, and to other
darker rites when a victim was slain as the personification of that spirit, to ensure a resurrection in
spring.   Even in Christian times, and before our
forefathers had freed themselves from the lingering
customs of paganism, they preserved the maiden as
an act of faith and religious duty.   What is now
a pleasant ending to the labours of the season was
formerly a serious fact, a rite which, if omitted,
might entail the entire subversion of the order of
nature for the season.   Formerly the god was
present among men, and could give or withhold
blessings, and on that account his rites could not be
neglected with impunity.   Man has travelled far in
his conceptions of divinity since then, but the facts
of the present connect the life and knowledge of
modern times with a long-forgotten past, which carries
us back to the youth of the world, when man first
began to make his way, by slow and painful steps,
to an understanding of the facts of the universe
around him, and the supernatural which he felt must
exist somewhere.   The significance of his acts has
changed, and the ideas which are associated with
them have no resemblance to what an earlier people

conceived, but the acts remain. They are the same substantially the world over. It is impossible they could have been so universally borrowed, and the only conclusion is, that they existed from earliest times.

CHAPTER IX

PROPHECY

THE office of magician is to primitive man what that of prophet is to a more advanced people. He is the teacher of the ignorant; he delivers to men the oracles of the gods; he foretells events, and explains what is mysterious. The term magician, as that is ordinarily understood, does not cover the idea savage man has regarding his religious teachers. His conception is that of one possessed of supernatural knowledge, wisdom, and power; power which he has in virtue of his office, and which he can exercise in the discharge of it. He is in reality what the prophets of Israel were to the Jews; so I adopt the terms prophet and prophecy rather than magician and magic.

Under witchcraft frequent reference was made to magicians and recognised diviners. These magicians, or prophets as we shall call them, are among primitive men a distinct class, who, dating their origin from the very beginnings of society, developed into guilds or colleges with the growth of thought and early human institutions. As man's conceptions of deity and the physical facts around him expanded, the necessity of special insight into the spiritual sphere was felt. The king was no longer the only god; he had ceased to be god at all; his father, and the fathers of countless thousands, passed in long array before the worshipper's imagination as objects of worship ; true divinities, whom he was bound to honour and obey on pain of dire physical calamity. But while under the necessity of doing homage to departed ancestors, he knew nothing of their condition, could hold no converse with them, nor ascertain their wants and wishes. The more he longed for a glimpse beyond the portals of this mortal life, the denser the darkness closed around him. The king, content with temporal power and a more secure tenure of office than in former days, left such matters to those who might find it more easy to quit the upper air, should the gods call. In any case, it was more convenient for him that they should enter the home of the gods, than that he himself should be compelled to change substantial and tangible honours, even if necessarily temporary, for those shadowy if permanent glories of which he knew little and understood less.

The circumstances demanded men of boldness of conception and clearness of vision. The necessities of the case were urgent, and could not be met by half measures or halting compromises. Men must know something of the unseen, and if their just aspirations were to be met, a new departure was the only alternative to the collapse of all institutions and the overthrow of the physical universe. This being the condition of society in those far-away times of transition, there is no doubt but the earlier prophets were simply men who could see farther than their fellows, and who, piecing together the meagre

philosophies of the past, boldly struck out a new
system, and appealed to men as the interpreters of
all that was essential and permanent in the past.
The temporary and passing they abolished, as they
understood it, while they retained what was truth
and permanent. At first their efforts would be
wholly devoted to giving an explanation of the facts
of life and natural phenomena as these from time to
time presented themselves. An attempt would be
made to reconcile man's original conception of deity
and providence with the changed conditions and
more advanced thought. For a time this would be
sufficient, and the religious teachers would flatter
themselves, as has so often been done in the history
of the church, that they had arrived at a complete
and final solution of all questions regarding both
gods and men. But this could not be. Fresh compli-
cations would arise, and each, as it pressed on men's
minds, necessitated fresh explanations. The successive oracles needed to be consistent with fact and with
one another, which, as they accumulated, they were
not. The prophets themselves needed to be inter-
preted as well as the facts they sought to explain.

Besides, new claimants would arise, outbidding the
old for popular favour and official recognition. The
office, at first hereditary, or at least confined to a
close guild or college, would become vulgarised as
dishonest or ignorant men found their way into
office. Apart from this, daring and speculative
spirits among the community would not be permanently silenced. Sooner or later their conclusions
would reach the multitude, and the new thoughts,

struggling for recognition, would compel the prophets to adjust their system to that which men had
discovered independently of their order. Should
the oracles delivered by two persons claiming the
prophetic gift differ, the bolder or less scrupulous of
the two would naturally assert that he had held
communication with the gods, and that his oracle
must be accepted as final. But this would establish
a dangerous precedent, and the next time a difficulty
arose his rival would be prepared with a revelation
at the initial stage. Here we have two elements
which would of necessity lead to a vast extension of
the order in point of numbers, and a great widening
of the scope of prophecy itself, tending to convert
what began as a philosophy into an occult art.
This in process of time would lead to a subdivision
of function ; one would become the prophet or doctor
of war ; another of rain ; a third of witchcraft ; a
fourth of lightning. The multiplication of offices
and prophets to fill them would be regulated by
man's necessities on the one hand, and his ability to
support such an army of ghostly councillors on the
other; these being periodically thinned out, when,
as in the case of the King of Babylon's vision, it was
made abundantly plain that the whole college was a
huge imposition and fraud.

If this is a correct or even probable explanation of
the origin and development of the office, it would be
natural to infer a steady and sustained deterioration
or degradation of the order both in character and
influence. And this is what we do find. For while
among those tribes farthest removed from civilisation

the prophet is sacred, and his every word received as the oracle of heaven, among those who have advanced in their philosophy a chief has been known to sacrifice his whole college in one holocaust. The King of Moreo, referred to in an earlier chapter, is a case in point. Nebuchadnezzar would have been another but for the timely intervention of Daniel; while we have recent examples in Zululand and in the country of Moselekatse of the same thing.

Nor is the explanation offered inconsistent with the history of the Jewish prophetic order as given in the sacred books of the Hebrews themselves. The older prophets are giants, men both before and above their time, and who left the impress of their own character on the life and institutions of their country. The later prophets, like the later judges, mark a fatal deterioration. Whole schools of them fell from their own standard of office, and sought to bear the name of prophet when everything but the name had perished. Those the sacred writers describe uniformly as " false prophets." They were men who sought office not because they had a message for men, but because they could calculate on the ignorance and credulity of the people for gain. To such prophets it is said : " Will ye pollute Me among My people for handfuls of barley and pieces of bread ? " * Not content with such imposition as false prophecy, as understood in their own day, they fell back on older superstitions, and appealed to lingering beliefs which had long passed away. They revived the primitive doctrines regarding human souls and the power of divine or sacred

* Ezek. xiii. 19.

persons over these; for it is made clear that, like
their ancestors in the primeval jungle, they professed
to catch and retain souls. "Woe to the women that
sew pillows to all armholes, and make kerchiefs upon
the head of every stature to hunt souls. Will ye hunt
the souls of My people, and will ye save the souls alive
that come unto you?"* Compare this with the
following account of a common custom in the South
Seas; "Two young wizards were passing a house
where a chief lay very sick; they saw a company
of gods from the mountains sitting in the doorway.
They were handing from one to another the soul of
the dying chief. It was wrapped in a leaf, and had
been passed from the gods inside the house to those
at the doorway. One of the gods handed the soul
to one of the wizards, taking him for a god in the
dark, for it was night. Then all the gods rose up
and went away; but the wizard kept the chief's
soul. In the morning some women went with a
present of very fine mats to fetch a famous phy-
sician. The wizards were sitting on the shore as
the women passed, and they said to the women;
'Give us the mats, and we will heal him.' So they
went to the chief's house. He was very ill; his jaw
hung down and his end seemed very near. But the
wizards undid the leaf, and let the soul into him
again, and forthwith he brightened up again and
lived."†

The false Hebrew prophets thus carry us back to
a practice which existed in early days—for wizards
could steal as well as restore—when souls were

* Ezek. xiii.   † J. G. Frazer, quoting G. Turner: *Samoa.*

hunted and caught ; a clear proof that the office had
fallen so low that its original conception was lost or
forgotten. Of this we shall see farther illustration
when considering the duties of prophets among
primitive men, and how these were performed
at various stages of culture during the world's
progress.

Every prophet claims to hold converse with the
world of spirits, and to act in discharge of his sacred
functions only in obedience to the will of the gods.
Does he carry the soul of a sick person back to
the invalid's bedside ? * It is because the gods
reveal to him that the sick is to recover. Does
he offer sacrifice for rain ? He does it to appease
the wrath of the offended ancestors, or because
they are hungry and are crying out for food.†
When he, by his arts, secures places and persons
against the thunderbolt, after being struck by
lightning, he assuages the anger of the gods, who
have visited their children with affliction because of
some neglect of filial duty. Should the prophet be
called upon to discover a witch or wizard, he "smells
them out"; but it is the gods who reveal to him who
they are, a knowledge which they deny to all others.

The subject of prophecy and magic is too wide for
full discussion in a single chapter, and can be best
illustrated by selecting one or two particulars, as the
treatment of the sick and the methods adopted to
detect crime. We have already seen the methods
by which wizards are detected when considering
the subject of witchcraft. Other criminals are

* Gill : *Myths and Songs of the South Pacific.*
† Hon. C. Brownlee, MS. Notes.

discovered by means of a magic horn.* This may be
the horn of a domestic sheep or that of an antelope,
and the prophet, by looking into it and examining
its contents, can discover a thief or murderer.   By
the same means he is supposed to know the whereabouts of the stolen property, if not removed beyond
the tribal boundaries—a necessary qualification in
this branch of the profession.   Readers of Highland
traditions will recognise in this the well-known
" second sight " of Celtic legend.   Those possessing
this gift could foretell events, especially deaths and
calamity, and in doing so used the shoulder-blade of a
sheep, through which they looked, and saw the future
in panorama before them.   I once met, at Paible,
North Uist, a man who was said to "see things."
The old man, who derived his living, partly at
least, from propitiatory gifts, had quite a reputation
for prophecy, and if he suggested to any one by a
dark hint that he had seen a shroud, that family
was plunged into grief, knowing that he referred to
one of their number, though no name was mentioned.

The prophet, among savage men, explains the
cause of drought and floods, and must devise a
remedy for these visitations.   Among the Zulu
tribes, if the spring rains are late, a black ox is sent
to the doctor, who being warned of the approaching
visit, sits in his hut covered with a thick layer of
mud.   If there are no indications of rain, he may
direct them to come after the lapse of a few days;
but if things are propitious, he at once orders a
muster of the tribe.   There is much feasting and
dancing, mystic ceremonies are performed, sacrifices

* Speke.

are offered, and then the prophet announces that
before a given day rain will fall. Should the prediction prove correct, well ; if not, the prophet must
account for his failure. This he does by charging
some one high in authority, as the chief's principal
wife, with working against him, and raising a dry
wind which drives the clouds away. This she does
by exposing her posterior to the skies.

In time of war the prophet has to perform rites to
ensure victory. Among the Waganda, when the
case is urgent, a child is flayed and placed on the
path, and the warriors made to step over it,* or a
child and a fowl are placed on a grating over a pot
with water in it. Another pot, inverted, is used as
a cover, and a fire kindled to heat the water. After
a given time the contents are examined, and if found
dead the war must be delayed as the omen is against
the expedition.†

But the prophet's services are not confined to the
living ; they extend to the dead. In Akra when
a young person dies the body is placed on a
bier. This is raised on two men's heads, and carried
to a place indicated by the prophet, who accom-
panies the procession. Arrived at the spot, he takes
his stand in front of the corpse. He holds in his
hand a magic reed, which he shakes over the body,
and at the same time asks the question, " Was your
death caused by age and infirmities ? " If this is
answered in the affirmative by the body impelling
the bearers forward, no more is said, and the funeral
proceeds ; if not, the prophet continues : " Was it
caused by your bad actions ? " Corpse answers

* Speke.   † *Ibid.*

"No" by remaining perfectly still. "By whose witch was it caused, so and so, or so and so?" naming the head men of the district.* When the right name is mentioned the dead impels the bearers forward. It is the duty of the head man indicated, or rather his magicians, to discover the culprit by the approved methods.

The dangers to the dead are not over when the soul has left the body, and the Angoni prophet must see to it that the devil, to use a Highland phrase, is cheated of his own. Did evil spirits know a man's grave in that unhappy land, they would undoubtedly steal his soul to be educated in their own evil college. So every precaution must be taken for the repose of the departed. Till burial the soul of an Angoni hovers near the body, seeking an opportunity to re-enter its former abode. A soul does not at first know death. To it death is sleep. " Death and sleep," said a Kaffir once to me, " are one word." This being the case, a lay figure is made before the funeral. At the hour announced this figure is carried out, followed by a great concourse of people, who weep and wail, mourning for the dead. As soon as the cortége leaves the house drums are beat, horns blown, and guns fired to drive away evil spirits. These, kept back by the noise, hover about the out-skirts of the crowd, lured on by the signs of mourn-ing, till the grave is reached. There the figure is buried with all the respect and honour due to the departed, and as the crowd disperse the devils swoop down upon the grave to snatch away the soul, but only to find they have been outwitted and betrayed.

* Winterbotham.

Meantime the corpse has been quietly and expe-
ditiously buried without beat of drum or sound of
horn.* By using such precautions the prophets
outwit the devil, and do an important service to the
dead and the ancestral spirits, who wait the arrival
of their brother spirit with much anxiety.

When a Wahunga chief dies, his prime minister is
killed and buried with him, to be his councillor in the
dangers of the passage. All his wives are also killed
except one. For her a pit is dug in the ground, just
large enough to hold her. In this she is placed and
covered over with earth, a small breathing aperture
being left. A spear is passed down this hole,
which she holds in her hand ; if at the end of
the second day she is alive and holds the spear, she
is taken out and allowed to live. If her fingers
are too nerveless to grasp the spear, no farther
ceremony is needed; she is buried already.†

The Congo natives keep the bodies of their chiefs
for years, wrapping them in successive layers of cloth
till the mass is so heavy as to be hardly portable.
The same was done in the case of the queen-mother
of Uganda, for whom Mackay made the famous
copper coffin, and with whom, within and around her
three coffins, £1500 worth of cloth and copper was
buried ; a fact which proves that the Waganda do
not wish royal personages to be restricted in the
matter of apparel in ghostland.

When King Eyambo (Congo) died, the prophets
ordered thirty of his wives to be burned the first
day,‡ and before the funeral rites were over several

---

* Dr. Elmslie, MS. notes.   † J. Thomson, *Through Masai Land*.
‡ Waddell.

hundreds were sent to accompany him. Should he have gone without a respectable following, or with only a few, the spirits would ask, " What poor slave is this who is coming alone ? " and on the discovery that it was a king, his people would be visited with every form of calamity for having allowed their monarch to go from them like an unknown waif.

Prophets regulate functions of government, and in some cases determine the succession to the throne. In Uganda three chiefs or councillors, who are magicians or semi-divine, elect the new king from among the late monarch's sons, and generally select a young son—if an infant so much the better— for the regency is theirs, and the younger the king the longer will be their term of office. The elder sons are kept in confinement till the heir is of age, and then burned, except two or three reserved with the view of keeping up the succession should the young king die without issue.* This, though in theory an excellent system to prevent disputes, was apt to lead to awkward consequences for the three who held the regency. A son, when his father fell sick, might retire to another tribe, and, returning suddenly seize supreme power and send the regents to join their late master. This was done by the Batetwa chief Dingiswayo,† who fled to the Cape Colony, to return in a few years to claim his rights with direst results to his rival's patrons.

Prophets experiencing such vengeance now and then, sought to secure their order against untimely accidents by organising guilds or colleges, the

* Wilson.   † G. M. Theal, *Boers and Bantu.*

members of which were regarded as sacred in virtue of their office. Under such a system a king might be slain by a rival, but the magicians were sacred, and their divinity would be respected. The rules of their order permitted them to be the supporters of the *de facto* king, apart from oaths of allegiance to one who might be a fugitive. Thus the Bulloms have an institution binding its members to keep the sacred mysteries secret for ever, and to yield prompt and unquestioning obedience to the superior of the order ; * rules which raise a doubt as to whether Loyola's conceptions were marked with that degree of originality which is generally attributed to them. New members are admitted after a long novitiate, during which the most severe tests are put upon their loyalty and resolution. Even then they cannot be admitted till friends of theirs, already members, bind themselves by an oath to put the novice to death instanter, should he make known any forbidden secret. The manner of execution is as secret as it is expeditious and effective. There is no escaping the ordeal of the guild. Similar institutions, with local modifications, exist among the Soosoms, Timmanes, Basutos, and many other tribes. Among the Timmanes a woman prophetess is general of the order, and a kind of inquisition or confessional exists among them. To the care of this hag fathers and husbands confide their daughters and wives, and the methods pursued by her and her college is highly characteristic. When a penitent appears she is smeared with white clay, and asked

* Winterbotham.

to confess, on pain of death. If her confession is deemed satisfactory she is dismissed with an admonition, and injunctions to perform certain acts, unless her sin is witchcraft, in which case she is sold into slavery. If any one refuse to confess, nothing more is heard of her. Should the confession be unsatisfactory in itself, a decoction is given to force a fuller statement from the penitent. This, if the confession was not full, causes intolerable pains which can only be relieved by the priestess. If pains follow, she proceeds to discover the concealed crime by means of divination. The penitent is then charged with it, and asked to plead. If she deny the crime, she is sold ; if she refuse to plead, she is poisoned.*

These guilds exist wherever religion has developed into a system. The chief priest assumes functions to himself which belong to royalty, and so reduces the kingly office to a shadow. This is the case with the Egbo of Calabar,† the Lubare of Uganda,‡ and the Moro of the Waneka.§ The same abnormal development of the power of the priestly office took place in Europe during the Middle Ages. The temptation and danger of all religious systems is to claim power and authority over men's lives and actions outside its own proper sphere. The result in such cases has always been a degrading of the sacred office, and ultimate disaster to the system itself.

But there is another permanent function of prophecy, important in itself, and universal among savage men, which has been touched upon only

* Winterbotham.   † Waddell.   ‡ Mackay.   § New.

incidentally, and that is foretelling the future.
When a tribe goes to war a great many details
cannot be arranged by the chief and his councillors ;
they must be determined by augury. Such details
seem to us to be of the very essence of practical
affairs, to be decided by generals, but to savage men
the case presents itself in an entirely different
aspect. The prophet must decide the strength of
the expedition, the clans who are to send their
contingents, the sacred place where the army is to
be charmed, and the route that is to be taken. Nor
can a general go into action, even against a handful,
should the oracles be unfavourable. In 1879, during
a period of disturbance in South Africa, a chief,
Umhlonhlo, was marching leisurely across country
with his whole army. The day was hot, and not a
cloud could be seen. Presently the magicians, ever
on the alert for omens, noticed a peculiarly shaped
cloud on the horizon. It rose rapidly in one mass,
and was observed " to roll upon itself." Its progress
was intently watched till it reached the zenith and
passed over the sun. This was an evil omen. The
spirits were offended, and had passed in shadow
over the chief and his army. Their backs were
turned upon their children. There was, however,
no immediate danger, for their scouts had reported
that no soldiers were within many miles of
their line of march, and they could retire to some
sacred spot to have their warriors re-charmed.
While they were discussing which place to resort
to, the van of a small column of cavalry appeared
unexpectedly over a rising ground. Dismay was

written on every countenance; black fear was in every heart. The war minister, one of the bravest of men, urged the troops to form into order of battle. No one answered his summons. A fatal paralysis had crept over chief and people. He did his best to organise an orderly retreat, but in vain ; not a blow was struck ; every man took to his heels, and the army never reassembled.

On another occasion a chief, Oba, led an army against some people of the Fingoe tribe. He knew their place of encampment, and sent a trusted spy to find out all he could and report. This man crept up close to their camp fires, and there saw a diviner pronouncing an incantation against Oba and his army. This was reported to the chief who paid no regard to it. But on the following morning two ospreys flew over the army uttering piercing cries. This the prophets declared to be an evil omen which boded defeat, but Oba was not to be frightened by Fingoe curses or the screams of birds, and advanced boldly. From the crest of a hill they saw the Fingoe camp, and a number of cattle grazing between. Six men tended the herd, and these advanced shouting "Basolieve," meaning " they are cursed." Qwarana was ordered to advance, which he did at the head of his men. When quite near the Fingoes fired a volley, shooting Qwarana through the body. This was enough ; the army turned and fled. Oba did his best to stay the panic ; he begged his soldiers to act like men, he called them cowards and women. It was in vain. They had been warned by the ospreys, and now a body of nearly two thousand warriors fled in panic before six cowherds.

But the future cannot be left to such accidents as a midday shadow, or the flight of eagles. Methods that can be resorted to at any time must be found. These differ among most tribes, but the following may be taken as illustrative. The Bongo consult the oracle thus :—A stool of a particular wood is made, the surface of which is rubbed perfectly smooth, a block of the same wood is then prepared to lie flat on the stool. When a response is wanted a few drops of water are placed between the stool and the block, the latter is then moved backwards and forwards. If it moves easily, and begins to glide without friction, the oracle is favourable ; if not, the undertaking proposed cannot prosper. Or an oily fluid from the bengeye-tree is given to a hen. If the bird dies there will be misfortune ; if not, success.* Another method, which the same observer records, is to dip a cock again and again in water till it is senseless. It is then left in the sun, and should it revive the augury is favourable. By such means men determine war and peace, as well as the guilt or innocence of accused persons.

The Bullom tribes determine the future by " casting the sand."† This may be to discover if a sick person is to recover or not. The diviner takes a goatskin on which he carefully spreads a layer of fine dry sand ; he then shuts his eyes, and with the three first fingers of his right hand makes lines and dots in the sand. According to the position of these, the

---

* Schweinfurth.   † Winterbotham.

patient will live or die. The same result may be obtained by taking a number of palm nuts, and arranging them in groups with the eyes closed. Gallas divine from the appearance of the entrails of slaughtered animals,* while almost every action a Basuto or Baralong performs is determined by the fall of dice. So it happens, that when a man goes to commit a crime, he lays aside his fetish, and does not consult the oracle, as he could not in that case obtain a favourable response. He covers his god with a cloth, that he may not know what the worshipper is doing.† The Wayao determine the future by a flour cone. When a man has determined on an undertaking, as a journey, his magician takes a quantity of flour, and lets it fall in a steady stream at the head of his bed. If it forms a perfect cone as it falls, the omen is good ; if not, that is an end of the matter by the flour-cone test. Should the cone be perfect, it is covered by an inverted pot and left for the night. In the morning, when the pot is removed, the cone is examined, and if found perfect, there is nothing further needed beyond offering the custo- mary sacrifice. But if there has been a falling down of the flour, even a small slip, it is a sign not to be disregarded. An equally effective method is to pour out beer on the ground, which if it sinks at one spot is a good omen, but if it runs along the ground, bad.‡ Three bits of stick may be laid on the ground, two parallel and one across. If found, after an interval of some hours, in position as left, the oracle has granted the worshipper's prayer.

---

* Krapf.   † Tucker.   ‡ Duff Macdonald.

When prophecy descended to such trivialities as those represented by the auguries and observances referred to, it was doomed as a system. While it contented itself with exposition, purgation of demons, expanding philosophic conceptions and the enunciation of principles in an abstruse form, it commanded men's respect, and the prophet was regarded as a divinely commissioned messenger. But when it descended to the petty details of village life, it could not escape the fate of any great institution which is hopelessly vulgarised. When the prophet became little better than the court fool he could only receive a fool's treatment. When a man who hurt his toe against a stump could command the services of the expounders of the supernatural to explain the fact, it was not surprising that other men, despising at once tree stumps and prophets, should introduce a new and more vigorous, if less reverent, form of government.

As men's conception of divinity expanded from the crude unformed idea of a divine king to local deities, reaching gradually towards one supreme god, the world needed a philosophy to correspond with the new-born faith. This, prophecy did not as a system supply. Instead of advancing with the growth of thought to a higher and truer conception of life, it pursued a course which could only lead to deterioration and final extinction. But though prophecy as a system became moribund, and so continues among savage men, it was from it the new philosophy took its rise. This philosophy springing out of what was once a system in advance of current thought, led to the development of the great religious systems which at different periods became world wide. While the old-world prophet " cast the sand," or fumbled among the entrails of an expiring cock, there were men among his disciples who conceived bolder notions, and only waited for a favourable opportunity to give practical effect to their thoughts. They had to wait many weary years, generations, centuries, but their opportunity came at last. Such men in the early days could do little beyond raising a protest against the most glaring abuses among their own order and in society. Even in this they would meet with treatment similar to that experienced by the Hebrew prophet Jeremiah, and many of them would share the fate of all bold reformers—the gallows or the fire. One after another would quietly disappear as unworthy of their office and subverters of the faith of men. But the ashes of such men do more to fertilise the soil of human thought than their wisdom while they live. Like the dragon's teeth, they produce a fresh and ever-increasing number of souls with like thoughts and aspirations. The words of such men are treasured by a few. They are pondered, digested, made fruitful of new thoughts. As the years pass, and the angry passions raised by the heretic's teaching die away, men first view him as one who meant well, next as a true prophet, and finally as a sacred being whose memory is cherished as a divine heritage. Posterity places him among the gods. He was incarnate.

No sooner is the popular mind led to regard such

men as saints and martyrs, than a web of romance is woven round their lives, and the philosophy they taught becomes a new religion. Those of their successors who cherish their memories and keep their teaching alive, seize the opportunity, and boldly claim divine sanction for their doctrine. This is one way. There is another. All such reformers do not share the martyr's fate. A powerful king, weary of the inanities taught and practised by his college of magicians ; weary too of the endless sacrifices and the ever-deepening stream of human blood ; blood it may be, as in the case of a king of Ashantee, in which to float the royal canoe,* throws the protection of his strong arm over the reformer, as the king of Babylon did to Daniel, and so encourages the movement. Or, it may be, the reformer, finding the current too strong, retires to a lonely place where he lives a life of meditation and privation. Such a man, especially after the invention of writing, formulates doctrines into aphorisms. These, brief, wise, practical, as they must be in his circumstances, he communicates to the few faithful disciples admitted to his sanctuary and confidence. They carry them from hamlet to hamlet, thence from house to house, where they pass into the current language of the people. These, when received with favour, the popular imagination connect with a direct revelation from the gods; ultimately it deifies the man who utters them.

Such a life as this would lead a man to introspection and a comparison between himself, with his

* Kühne.

half-uttered wisdom, and the folly of popular beliefs. There was nothing more natural than for him to conclude that he was god-possessed, and that his words and actions were those of the god. When this was asserted and boldly proclaimed, men in a primitive age, when the old order and the worship of ancestral spirits was discredited, and the new still unsettled and fluctuating, would readily seize upon the idea as giving a clue to the solution of the perplexities with which they were surrounded. The very multiplicity of ancestral gods complicated the situation. The presence of demons, as powerful and more subtle than the gods themselves, made matters worse. The great, or one god, was too shadowy and remote to be approached, and his existence, if he did exist, gave no relief to the pious. Thus the incarnation of divinity, in the person of a prophet, would be hailed as giving a hope that the mysteries of the spirit world would at length be solved.

But we are now approaching a stage of development which carries us beyond the bounds of our inquiry. In Africa there has been no great incarnation of deity as in Brahmanism and in Buddhism. An examination of these, however brief, would lead to the discussion of Vedic religion, which is foreign to my present purpose. The fact to be noted is, that earlier forms led to the incarnation of the founders of the respective systems, and that myth surrounded them with a halo which makes it impossible to distinguish the true from the false, so as to get at the man and the philosophy he taught in its simplicity and truth. For it is the truth which those systems contained that has given them vitality to exist through so many thousands of years.

Thus, from the rude conception of a divine king who ruled nature, thought advanced to a doctrine of souls, thence to separate and personal divinities, slowly gravitating towards the idea of one supreme god, unknown and unknowable. Pursuing its inquiries, never resting for a moment, the human mind reached the conception of the one god becoming incarnate in time. And here it is curious to note, that those in whom deity became incarnate, so far as we can discover, put forward comparatively modest claims, and that these were expanded by their disciples into a cumbrous mass of doctrinal teaching which, in some cases, fell to pieces by the very weight of its ritual and ordinances. Men could not bear the burden.

In Africa, always excepting ancient Egypt and the countries bordering upon it, there is nothing which corresponds with the Asiatic development of religion. The art of writing being unknown would, apart from other causes, have made that impossible. But our inquiries have, so far, tended in the direction of a development not unlike that through which the great systems of the east must have passed. Tradition does not preserve the words of wise men, as is done where there is a literature. The words may be said to remain, or a faint echo of them, but tradition gives them a local setting and myth adapts them to local circumstances. Still, the position occupied by the God of the Wayao, as the God of the original inhabitants, and his reputation as a beneficent and powerful deity, points to a deification of a prophet whose soul was developed into a principal god. Mlungu is doubtless such another. A great man whose memory has waxed dim, and whose words cannot be recalled as those of Brahma may. Myth itself has almost died away in the course of ages, yet Mlungu lives as a faded memory though the traditions of his life have perished.

The sketch attempted of the growth and decay of the prophetic order is consistent with what we are familiar with. In a highly developed state of society the prophetic function ceases to be exercised as we meet with it in primitive times. But it is still present. The wise men of a nation are its prophets. Its poets, philosophers, preachers, reformers, scientists, and discoverers, are as truly the guides of men's thoughts and actions as were the magicians of Ancient Egypt or Chaldea. They are the descendants of humble ancestors who determined the fate of individuals and nations by casting the sand, or by the spots found on the entrails of a decapitated cock. Men may imagine themselves independent of all external circumstances, but we are the creatures of our surroundings as were those who sacrificed their god that his spirit might enter his successor. We may make it our boast that we have freed ourselves from the thraldom of superstition, but there are still curious survivals among us. And of these, one of the most remarkable is the suspicion with which religious teachers are regarded in popular imagination.

There is a deeply rooted prejudice against religious teachers among the peasantry of Europe, and not unfrequently those who are most devout in the discharge of their own religious duties, have the most pronounced superstitions regarding clergymen. Fishermen will not go to sea with a minister on board, as in that case no success would attend their labours; they will not even have one enter their boats, if possible, as that is apt to take the boat's luck away. Skippers fear to have them as passengers, and voyagers expect contrary winds if a priest should happen to be among their fellow voyagers. I remember one, Rob MacLauchlin, the owner of a smack that plied between Oban and Morven, having on one occasion a very boisterous passage, to the intense alarm of his passengers. On his arrival one of the villagers remarked on the state of the weather and how suddenly the storm had sprung up. Rob, who had had a sail carried away and was in no good humour, replied, garnishing his sentences with expletives which I shall omit, "How could we escape wind with three ministers on board." These worthies were on their way to a local meeting of Presbytery. One of them, ignorant of seamen and their ways, offered a remonstrance, and tried to enlighten the skipper, but had to beat a hasty retreat. Rob knew all about it by long experience, and all his predecessors, from the days of Jonah at least, had been conversant of the fact. That was final and admitted of no appeal, and the villagers to a man sympathised with the skipper who was compelled to carry such cargo.

Nor is this fear confined to traditions of the sea. The minister is feared because he can bless or ban, and village children regard him as a being to be avoided when that is possible. When at play, if he happens to pass, there is a hurried and fearful whisper of "There's the minister," and play ceases till he is well out of reach. If they must present themselves before this august presence, they cease to be children as by instinct, and a word or movement becoming the age of five or six meets with the awful maternal reproof, "Do ye no ken that's the minister?" Clergymen themselves are, perhaps, largely to blame. The Church has played so many parts on the stage of European politics and social life that much of the present suspicion may be owing to her arrogance and avarice. But this is not all. Like our harvest customs, this superstitious reverence and fear, is doubtless a survival from primitive times, when the magician was a being to be at once feared and honoured. The primitive man who offended one of those powerful beings who directed all his life's actions, might expect to be the next victim when a case of witchcraft had to be disposed of, or, if no case cropped up the gods might require his presence among them, and so demand him as a sacrifice. And so it is that in spite of respectability, unblemished reputation, great services to mankind, honour, place and influence, religious teachers have never been able to free themselves from the suspicion and fear with which their humble ancestors, the priests of the jungle, were regarded in popular imagination.

This is perhaps an extreme instance of the persistency of early beliefs, but it goes to show how slowly
the human mind parts with ideas once universal,
and the vast intervals that must elapse before a
complete revolution in thought is possible under the
most favourable circumstances. There could be no
condition more likely to obliterate the past than
that created by Christianity, and yet these customs,
myths, and superstitious fears have lived through
millenniums of literature and careful oral teaching.
The process has been slow, and is not yet completed.
And what has taken Europe from the dawn of
history to accomplish, with the aid of literature,
philosophy and Christianity, could not be done
by the African groping his way through oral
tradition and universal usage through many
thousands of years. The customs which we study
to-day, and which at first sight appear to be local
or tribal, carry us back in their original form to a
period long anterior to the first dawn of traditional
history in the East. They bring us into contact
with the condition of the world before the families
of men began to scatter themselves hither and
thither over the face of the earth. They are our
only record of the condition of the world when it
was young, and of man in his first struggles with
the problems with which he found himself surrounded as he began to look out upon the works of
nature as these could be seen in his immediate
locality.

CHAPTER X

SOCIAL USAGES

IT may at first appear as if there were no connection between the religion of primitive peoples and their social usages. The latter, according to European ideas, have so little of the nature of religious rites that they are seldom associated with piety and devotion to the gods. Some men spend their lives among savages and never look below the surface, nor do they suspect that those whom they daily meet have any forms of religious observance. I was once told by a missionary of twenty years' standing in Africa that certain ceremonial acts performed by natives had no religious significance. In fact, he went so far as to say, " These people have no religion; they live a purely animal existence; whatever they do is just custom." How the worthy man, for he was a truly pious soul, could ever get into sympathy with them, or make any impression upon their minds, I have often wondered. I have long ceased to wonder how a man of such unblemished life and absolute devotion to duty, but so totally blind to the facts of savage life, should have to confess with a sigh and the shadow of a life's sorrow, that " the people about here are very hardened; few of them have come under the influence of the Gospel. It is very sad, and I at times doubt if I should be here, but I try to labour on in faith." Being at the time a novice in Africa, I accepted both statements without question. Since then I have learned a good deal, and among other things, that my aged friend's faith must have often been sorely tried as he endeavoured to do his duty in a sphere that never could have been congenial, but having made the mistake of becoming a missionary, he heroically stuck to the guns he had not learned the art of using. To gain any influence over savages one must first of all master their system of thought, and learn how to connect the most trivial acts with their philosophy, and such conceptions as they have of the supernatural. It is impossible to know what an act of devotion is till one has learned something of social usage and myth. To illustrate.

When a Dongolowa belle is to be married the eligible young men assemble, each armed with a kurbach or slave-whip. The elders of the tribe and a number of women gather as spectators and judges of the contest that is to follow. The young men, stripped stark naked, begin a mutual process of flogging, and he who stands this ordeal best is the successful wooer.* No other consideration or feeling is allowed to interfere with custom, as that would be displeasing to the gods. Should a woman marry without such a contest,-her prospects would be poor indeed, having despised an ordinance of heaven. At times there is a tie between two young men in the flogging match, and in that case the girl has to

* Felkin.

decide the matter between them. This she does, not by choosing one, for that would be to despise another equally worthy suitor whose hide in the end might prove the toughest. The matter must be decided in a more excellent way. It is done thus :— The coy maiden straps a knife to each of her arms, the blades projecting an inch or two below her elbows. She then sits down on a log, a suitor on either side sitting close beside her. At a given signal she raises her arms from the elbows, and leaning slowly forward rests her weight upon the young men's thighs, into which she steadily presses the knife blades. He who does not wince, or winces least under the ordeal, wins the bride and carries her off triumphant.

In Unyoro, the relatives of the late king fight for the throne. Here, too, it is a case of the toughest skin, but it is no vulgar contest, but a sacred function conformable to the will of the gods who delight in manly vigour. A Mitto chief warns those entering his country of war being made upon them, should they persist, by displaying on a tree near the path, an ear of corn, a feather and an arrow.* He who touches corn or cock will receive an arrow. In that country, too, a man wishing to marry applies to his chief for a wife. If thought worthy one is bestowed upon him, as all persons and property within the territory belong to the king. Both Mitto and Niam-Niam bury their dead, with strict regard to the points of the compass; men being buried with the face towards the east; women looking to the west.†

* Schweinfurth.   † *Ibid.*

This is conformable to the rule that women must eat alone, and not come near men at meals, unless it be to attend upon them. When a Waneka arrives at the age of puberty, he is smeared with white clay and decorated, after which he betakes himself to the woods, either alone or in company with others of his own age. There they must remain till they meet and kill a man, after which they wash off their clay and return home to be feasted and honoured.* They are now men, not boys. A Waneka prophetess begins operations at midnight by frantic screams. When all are astir she declares, "Roma, *i.e.*, spirit or the god, is here, and demands the sacrifice of a black ox." This is at once provided, and men heave a sigh of relief to find it is not a more costly victim.

The men of Jagga spit on a departing guest as an act of courtesy, and to bid him God speed. By so doing, they bestow on him their highest mark of honour, for it is a religious act. A Wakamba must carry away his bride by strategy, and for this purpose may have to lie in wait for months. Before he begins his vigil he pays the parents the dower. Hottentots preserve a certain membrane at birth, a bit of which is worn through life. Its loss would entail evil here and hereafter.† Common people in Dahomey may not grow grain except for domestic purposes, as all property belongs to the king. So, too, the persons of his subjects. At certain annual festivals he holds a sale of marriageable young women.‡ Court favourites receive wives free, but all others pay. Unlawful wounding is an injury done

* Krapf.　　　　† Moody.　　　　‡ Rowley.

to the king's person in that of his subject. All things merge in him as the head of the State and the object of reverence. To his people he is divine.

The house of the Bodio or high priest of the Kroomen is a sanctuary to which criminals may flee for refuge. From it they cannot be removed except by his orders, and, as he gives no reason for his decision, he shelters a large number of ruffians, who, more secure under his protection than ever Jew was in a city of refuge, live and enjoy themselves, doing all the dirty work and throat-cutting for the Bodio in their nightly prowlings. A Manganga magician, or even wizard, can soar aloft on the wings of the wind like a Highland beldam on her broomstick. The prophet among the same people can discover a criminal in the following manner. He calls a muster of the tribe, and then taking a bundle of reeds in his hand rushes round the circle of the assembled tribesmen. If the criminal is among them, one of the reeds flies out of his hand as he approaches him. This reed he picks up, as the magic reed, and lays the bundle aside. He then presses it against the man indicated, when, if he is guilty, the rod revolves in his hand.* When an earthquake occurred at Accra, the king issued a proclamation that his father's spirit was giving the earth a shake, because the children were not obeying the customs, and giving due reverence to the reigning monarch. After this, he called for three of his principal chiefs, gave each a drink of rum, delivered to them a message for his father to the effect that his wishes would be attended

* Elmslie, Krapf, Perry.

to, and then had them beheaded. Thirty-four others were enclosed in jar-like baskets, their heads projecting from the neck. These were brought in one by one and promptly beheaded, to go as an escort with the chiefs who carried the king's dutiful message. He then retired to his gardens, satisfied he had done an act of most reverent devotion. His conduct will not seem so strange and horrible as at first sight appears, when it is borne in mind that as late as 1230 human sacrifices were offered in Prussia in honour of the goddess of corn and fruits.*

When old King Chop of Calabar drank, a chief held his great toe. The chief of Old Town kept his soul in a sacred grove near a spring of water. Some Europeans, in frolic or ignorance, cut down part of the grove, to the intense indignation of the spirit, who, according to the king, would visit them with all manner of evil.† A successor is not chosen till the king is buried and all the ceremonies completed. These are elaborate and protracted. What becomes of the soul in the grove I do not know ; probably it enters the new king, who in turn deposits it in the wood for safe keeping. For, after all, this is the great object of savage man in guarding divinity, and if a perfectly safe place could be found for the purpose of depositing the soul there, he would be supremely happy. But as love laughs at locksmiths, so do wizards at man's arts in concealing the whereabouts of souls. To enter the council of government among the Waneka, the candidate is placed in an enclosure where he lies down as if stone dead. His head is

* Dr. Maclear.   † New.

then covered with a thick layer of mud. A mixture of clay and hair is spread over his face. Horns are mounted over his eyes, and his body decked with feathers. He is then led to the edge of the forest, where he wanders till he has killed a man, after which he returns and has a ring of rhinoceros hide placed upon his arm as a badge of office and to indicate that he is now a sacred person.* Some tribes regard twins as the greatest good luck, others as monsters to be killed—the harbingers of calamity. Most, if not all Africans have some sacred animal which they do not kill, and with which their lives are in some way bound up. This is in reality fetish, totem or clan badge, according to the stage of civilization at which a people has arrived. Among the Majame strangers are received in the following manner :—A goat is brought forward by the tribal priest, which the chief takes by the horns and spits on its forehead, saying, "As this stranger has come into our land, and says he is our friend ; if he lies may he perish, he and all his caravan." The stranger then takes the goat, and doing as the chief has done, says, "If I practise any evil against Maganine, him or his people, his cattle or his lands, may I utterly perish, and this caravan." † The goat's head is then cut off "that blood and saliva may mingle." The skin of its forehead is divided into two parts and one given to each of the parties to the contract. A small slit is made in this and worn as a ring on the middle finger in token of brotherhood. The Wagorengo of the same region practise blood brotherhood to

* New.   † Myer.

cement friendship.* The people of Kiwendo never
sacrifice a goat, but at their great religious meetings
they turn one adrift to wander where it will. The
animal has a collar of cowries tied round its neck, by
which it is distinguished from a strayed animal.†
This is the only approach to the idea of a scapegoat,
as understood by the Jews, I know of in Africa.
The goat is devoted to Lubare. Of old, when a
Scottish king gave an unjust judgment his neck
took a twist, and so remained till justice was done.
African chiefs have boils ‡ in such a case as this.

These customs I have set down at random, selecting them from the observances of peoples widely
apart. My object is not to trace the development
of any idea, but to show that all these are in the
savage mind associated with religion and the
worship of the gods. This will be better understood
if we now consider acts of devotion, and the object
aimed at by the performance of these acts.

* Ashe.   † *Ibid.*   ‡ Grant Stewart.

CHAPTER XI

ACTS OF DEVOTION—MYTHS

To the savage who is constantly surrounded with spiritual beings, and whose life is dependent on securing their continued favour, no actions can be performed without a religious significance. He has not arrived at the idea of natural law apart from agents which regulate phenomena. To these agents he owes allegiance, because of the benefits he receives at their hands, and according to his conceptions of their wants and wishes, their tastes and fancies, will his life and actions be ordered. At first sight it would appear as if the whole business of religion were left to its avowed professors, for these are in evidence in connection with every event which happens. But there could be no greater error than to conclude that the magician's vocation represents the domestic religious life of the people. We may take it as a general rule that the magician's services are required only in connection with what is unusual in village life, as births, marriages, deaths, accidents, evil omens or any circumstance the meaning of which may be doubtful. The religion of ordinary life, of eating and drinking, sleeping and walking, working and talking is conducted by each individual according to the approved method of the tribe. In

the details of this religion he has been instructed
from childhood. His intellectual faculties lie dormant, but the ritual of life has been burned into his
very soul and become part of his being. An
African is no more likely to forget the minutest
detail of private devotion than a European is to
forget to undress when he retires to rest. The
chief, as in the case of the Barotsi, may be a demi-
god,* and his people flock to his village for protection
during a thunderstorm, but it would be an error to
suppose the Barotsi devoid of a religion and ritual,
because of this simple childish trust in the divinity of
the chief. They have a peculiar method of presenting their offerings. A sacred horn is stuck into the
ground, and when they sacrifice they pour the blood
of the victim over the horn. It is also customary
to tie pieces of cloth devoted to the gods round it.
The horn is generally placed in a sacred grove, and
is really an altar to which the worshipper repairs to
do his private devotions.†

There seems but little religion in a number of
love-sick swains battering one another with slave
whips, nor in a maiden running knife-blades into
their thighs, but in a land where the bull is the
emblem of universal life the gods rejoice to see a
display of vigour and virile power. That and heroic
endurance are the cardinal virtues. A free fight
with bare sabres for a crown is not consistent with
our ideas of succession, and the suggestion of
weapons of war banishes all thoughts of devotion
from our minds. But he who is to sit upon the

* Arnot, *Garanganze*.   † *Ibid.*

throne favoured by the gods must, as an act he owes to them, win his position by giving evidence of the physique as well as mental vigour necessary for upholding the dignity of the tribe. A chief hanging on to the toe of old King Chop as he regaled himself with trade rum is not suggestive of altars and incense, but then King Chop himself was divine and represented the god-life to his people. To hold his toe was a sacred office, an act of dutiful obedience to the gods. Who could tell but, as he poured the "devil water" down his throat, the god spirit might escape by his toes if these were not held by a sacred person? The Waneka who wandered in woods with murderous intent during his novitiate believed himself to be doing a religious duty of the most sacred nature, and that without this preliminary the gods would never give him wisdom in council nor strategy in war. By obedience he was qualifying himself to advise regarding the affairs of gods and men, so different are savage man's conceptions of qualification for office from ours.

The King of Dahomey while doing homage to the gods would to us appear to be engaged in a profitable commercial transaction, and but for his being himself divine there would be a strong suspicion that considerations of profit influenced him. All the women of the country are his by divine right. It is an act of divine favour to bestow a wife on a subject, and when he does bestow one he expects handsome black mail. It is he who gives to men all they possess. They must toil for the corn which

the king gives through regulating the course of
nature, and if they must pay by toil for the lower
gifts, it would be impiety not to labour also for the
higher—that is, for their wives. The king has
given his subjects fecundity; they in return must
reward him for the blessing, else the younger generation of women will be barren.

Thus we see that many acts, which according to
Western ideas are far removed from the region of
devotion and worship, are in reality parts of a life
every act, word, and movement of which has a significance in a religious sense. I have seen natives of
Africa perform acts of devotion before the eyes of
men who declared that they had no idea of worship
nor of gods. When a native glances at the sun or
moon, he prays; when he drops a small particle of
food on the ground before he begins to eat, he offers
an oblation; if he throws a tuft of grass, a bit of
stick, or a stone, out of his hut door in the morning
before he emerges himself, he has said matins.
Nor does he neglect to sing vespers when he turns
his face to the bright constellations overhead before rolling himself up in his skin blanket for the
night. These are all acts of devotion, and represent
forms of worship common among a large proportion
of primitive men. They are performed by each
individual on his own account, apart from the more
formal religious rites which are the proper functions
of the magician. And this is consistent with what
we know of the growth of religious ritual among
those nations where the evolution of religion can be
best studied. The earliest forms of devotion of

which we have an account among the Jews were very simple and acts of sacrifice were exceptional and rare. With the development of the religious life of the people different orders sprung up, and these confined themselves to particular functions. But though we know but little of domestic and individual religion among the mass of the people, such indications as we have go to show that each man did perform acts of devotion however simple these might be.

We have seen that the king of Old Town kept his soul in a sacred grove, and that this was an act of devotion. It, however, gives the clue to a class of myths which are common from the Ganges to the Atlantic, and that is the soul dwelling apart from the body. It is difficult to classify the legends and folk-lore tales in which these myths are met with. They partake of magic certainly; but are more of the nature of devotion, and the caring for the soul's welfare by placing it in such safe keeping as to defy the enemies of mankind to obtain access to it.

In a former chapter reference was made to the soul's absence during sleep or fainting. Some of the dangers of soul-snatching by ghosts, wizards, and evil spirits have also been noticed. The dangers of the soul during its temporary absence were considerable. While resident in a man's body it was comparatively safe; but even then there were dangers, and dangers of such nature as to be difficult to guard against. While a man remained in sound vigorous health his soul was safe, but should he be taken ill his soul was then in danger, for it could be reached and injured, perhaps stolen, through his body, as in the case of the soul which the wizard got as it was handed about among the gods at the sick man's door. This being an admitted and recognised fact, it would be of the utmost importance for a man to have a place of safe keeping where he could deposit his soul in time of danger, and if this place were very secure, it would be a manifest advantage to have his soul kept there permanently. This would make a man independent of wizards on the one hand and of magicians on the other. The former could no longer hurt him ; the latter he could dispense with when freed from the fear of witchcraft. Such a man could boldly strike out a new course, and become a reformer by a defiance of the powers of evil, and a total neglect of the gods. Hence it is that such men, in popular imagination, are regarded as giants, monsters of impiety, cruel and cunning, regardless of all interests except their own, and oppressing all who come into their power. Evidence of this is found in the folk-lore tales taken from the traditions of peoples living widely apart, and the number and variety of such tales is proof that, at one time, this was a sober belief widely diffused throughout the world, and is a faithful reflection of the facts of life, in relation to the unseen, as these appeared to primitive man. These tales would in the first instance be preserved and recited as a true statement of the facts, and, handed down through millenniums of years, told at one time to warn the impious, at another as nursery rhymes, or by the fitful light of a blazing log on a winter's night, to amuse the curious, they would preserve much of their original form, though places and circumstances would change.

Such was the story of "Headless Hugh," of my own nursery days. I still, when the winds howl about the gables and among the trees, find my mind running back to the time when Headless Hugh was a real living man, who on stormy nights rode along the sea shore "between wave and sand," and watched whether little boys went to sleep quietly. If they did not he took them away on "the grey filly that never had a bridle." It must be nearly thirty years since I heard old Betty Miles tell the story. I could repeat it word for word now, so persistent are the impressions of childhood, especially when accompanied by a wholesome state of terror.

Hugh was a prince of Lochlin, and was long held captive by a giant who lived in a cave overlooking the Sound of Mull, and known by his name to this day. For many years Prince Hugh lived in the dismal recess of this grotto. One night there was a violent altercation between the giant and his wife, and Hugh who lay very still listening, knowing that he would be killed and eaten if it was known that he overheard their conversation, discovered that the giant's soul was in a great pearl—literally precious gem—which he always wore on his forehead. The prince watched his opportunity, seized the pearl, and having no means of escape or concealment, hastily swallowed the gem. Like the lightning from the clouds, the giant's sword flashed from its scabbard and flew between Hugh's head and his body to intercept the gem before it could be swallowed. It was too late, and the giant fell down, sword in hand, and expired without a gasp. Hugh had lost his head, but having the giant's soul in his body, saved his life and gained his liberty. He took the giant's sword, slew his wife, and then with the trusty weapon buckled to his side he mounted " the grey filly that never had a bridle, and swifter than the east wind," and made his way home unconscious of the loss of his head. His friends did not recognise him, declared he was a ghost, and refused to admit him to the palace, and so " he wanders in shades of darkness for ever, riding the grey filly faster than the east wind." On stormy nights he is seen riding along the shore " between waves and sand." He has taken many boys who would not go quietly to bed, and none of them have ever returned. This is the outline of a story I often heard from an old beldam who made my young life a long-continued torment while she had the opportunity of doing it.

Compared with it, the following Hindoo tale betrays a common origin in the days when such facts were soberly believed. The story is of a giant or magician who had held a beautiful queen captive for twelve years. At last the queen's brother came to visit her, and they both spoke the magician fair. He told them, in a moment of confidence, that he kept his soul thousands of miles away in a desolate country covered with jungle. In this jungle there was a circle of palm trees ; within the circle six water tanks, piled one above another ; under the lowest a birdcage with a small green parrot in it.

The parrot was his soul, or rather he kept his soul in the parrot. The queen's brother hearing this sought out the jungle, and at last found the cage which he brought to the magician's palace. When the magician saw it, he cried, " Give me my parrot." The boy tore off a wing ; the magician lost an arm. In this way he was torn limb from limb, and, finally, when the parrot's neck was wrung he fell down dead, his neck broken.* In another Hindoo story the soul is in a necklet. In a well-known Highland story the giant says : " There is a great flagstone under the threshold ; under the flagstone is a wether ; in the wether's belly is a duck ; in the duck's crop an egg, and that egg contains my soul." † The egg, as usual, is found and crushed and the captive is set free. The giant dies, of course.

The same form of superstition and myth is common to Teutons, Norse, Slavonians, Ancient Greeks, and Jews. The history of Samson, ‡ as recorded in the Book of Judges, is a case in point. He remained invulnerable till, through the wiles of his wife, he was shorn of his locks, and then his strength departed. The variations in this case from the Hindoo and Celtic tales is nothing more than might be expected, when the national characteristics of the Jews and their peculiar history is taken into account. This form of myth is as wide as humanity. I was on one occasion sitting in a Hlubi chief's house waiting for the appearance of the great man, who was doing his toilet, to hold a palaver. Several of his chiefs and

* Mary Frere, *Old Deccan Days.*   † Campbell.   ‡ Judges.

councillors were present, and entered freely into conversation with my attendants. I did not pay any particular attention to what passed till one of my own people said, in English, " Ntame has his soul in these horns," at the same time pointing to a pair of magnificent ox-horns placed in the roof by the lightning doctor to protect the house and its inmates from the thunderbolt. The horns were those of an animal offered in sacrifice and were sacred. I took the statement at the time to mean that to hold a palaver with Ntame was equivalent to holding converse with an ox, and made no farther inquiries. Whether my factotum spoke a parable, or stated a sober fact gathered from the councillors present, I cannot say. He addressed me in English, which he spoke fluently, and as no one else present understood a word of what he said I took his statement to be a hint to be careful what I said, and how I received our host's promises and professions of friendship. I have had no opportunity of verifying the statement, but the idea is in no way foreign to South African thought. A man's soul there may dwell in the roof of his house,* in a tree, by a spring of water, or on some mountain scaur.

This form of superstition leads by an easy transition to totemism, and it is on this account I regard it as more religion than magic or witchcraft. The object where the soul dwells is sacred, and it gets its sanctity because it is the home of the soul. This may be a bird, as the tufted crane among Kaffirs ; an animal, as the crocodile, among Bechuanas ; an insect,

* J. Sutton, MS. notes.

as among the Hottentots, who regard the *mantis
religiosa* as a divinity.   All these objects are sacred
because either a person's life is bound up with a
particular specimen, or the tribal life with a class.
The horns of a lightning sacrifice are sacred, and
must not be touched except by the doctor, but this
does not extend beyond the family in whose interests
the sacrifice was offered, while animals that are
sacred to the tribe are sacred to each individual
member of it.   To shoot a crane would be a more
heinous offence than to shoot a fox before the
hounds.   Again, tribes are named after animals or
objects, as the elephant people, the swimmers, men
of the wood, and such other names or titles de-
scriptive of supposed qualities as tradition has
preserved.

In Sutherlandshire at the present day there is a
sept of Mackays known as "the descendants of the
seal."   These claim as their ancestor a laird of
Borgie, who married a mermaid, and as the legend
has never been in print, I give it here as recently
told me by one well versed in north-country
mythology.*   It is as follows :—The laird was in the
habit of going down to the sea rocks under his castle
to bathe and drink salt water.   One day he saw a
mermaid close in shore, combing her hair and
swimming about as if anxious to land.   After
watching her for a time, he noticed her cowl on the
rocks beside him, and knowing she could not go to
sea without it he carried it up to the castle, hoping
she would follow him.   This she did ; but he refused

* Rev. A. Mackay.

to give up the cowl and detained the maid herself, whom he made his wife. To this she consented with great reluctance, and told him her life was bound up with the cowl, and if it rotted or was destroyed she would instantly die. The cowl was placed for safety in the centre of a large hay-stack, and there it lay for years. One day, during the master's absence, the servants were working among the hay and found the cowl. They showed it to the lady of the house, not knowing what it was. She took it, and then, strapping her child securely in its cot, she left and went to sea never to return again to Borgie. For years she used to come close in shore that she might see her boy, and then she would weep because he was not of her own kind so that she might have him at sea with her. The boy grew to be a man, and his descendants have always been exempt from drowning. They are famous swimmers, and are known locally to this day as " Sliochd an roin," that is, the descendants of the seal.

It is difficult to give an explanation of such myths as this, but when I first heard it I began to make inquiries, and discovered that there are floating traditions of shipwrecked crews having settled down among the native population, and I have thought that the Borgie mermaid may have been a cast-away maiden. If so, was she detained against her will? Did she make her escape? Were there negotiations about the custody of her child between her friends and the wild septs of the Reay country? And did local tradition weave these facts into the legend as it was current half a century ago? An

answer to these questions is made all the more difficult by the existence of other local traditions. There
is a sept known as " the men of the hide " in the
same district, and the tradition regarding their
name, if not their origin, is this :—The devil visited
the district to get the names of all those who were
willing to aid him. The laird of Cobachy met the
stranger, whom he found a "nice-spoken gentleman,"
albeit he was attired in a bull-hide with the horns
attached. The laird noticed that his visitor kept
his feet concealed, but in leaping a bog he got a
glimpse of the cloven hoof, and to get rid of him
recommended a visit to Melness. The devil put
to sea in his bull-hide, and raised the Kyle of
Tongue into foam and furrow as he crossed. After
an interval he returned, and called to pay his
respects to his friend Cobachy. The latter asked
how he had succeeded. " Oh," said he, " that is
the place to go to ; I have covered my hide with
names. I got so many that some are marked on
the horns."* The men of the district are known
as Fir-na-Sioch—the men of the hide. This the
present generation resent, and are apt to fly to their
fists if bull-hides are mentioned.

* Rev. A. Mackay, MS. notes.

CHAPTER XII

WOMAN

IN any inquiry into the religion of primitive men, it is necessary, if we are to understand the significance of many actions and familiar customs, to take account of woman's position and her true sphere in savage life. Many travellers describe woman among untutored tribes as a beast of burden pure and simple; an animal to be driven while it lasts and can do useful work; then left neglected to die, sometimes of hunger, but oftener by means still more equivocal. There could be no greater error than to accept such statements as correct, or as giving a clue to woman's position and influence among the community. That labour, which, according to western ideas, belongs exclusively to men, falls to the lot of women is true. Nor do they have a voice in village councils and palavers. Even domestic arrangements as brewing beer, the food for the day, washing and the like are regulated by the men, but this is largely accounted for by the system of polygamy. It is, however, this outward and apparent position of woman, which makes her appear to the stranger of so little consequence in the affairs of the community. She seems to be a mere drudge; a beast of burden with intelligence, and whose duty it is to

labour for her husband; bear children and rear them,
but take nothing to do with the produce of her own
labour or the training of her offspring.

We have already seen the prophetess at her work
in the Lake Region. We might find a woman
regent in South Africa. The wife of the noted chief
Makoma acted as regent during the minority of her
son, Sandili, and with conspicuous success. A
woman was once war doctor to Hintsa, and among
the Khonds a woman is not supposed to be unworthy
of representing the god life of creative energy and
reproduction. But it is more in the code of restrictions or taboos to which women are subject that we
learn the important place assigned to them in the
moral and religious codes of savage men. Individual women rising to eminence might prove too much
if that were taken by itself, but when we place such
facts beside the general treatment they receive, we
see how important is the place they occupy and the
influence they have on national life and religion.
For example. Among the objects placed under taboo
is blood, and especially woman's blood. So great is
the dread of its touching any part of the person,
and especially the head, which, in savage philosophy
is peculiarly sacred, that an Australian will not pass
under a leaning tree or the rails of a fence lest a
woman should have been on it, and that blood from
her, resting on the tree, might fall on him.* The
Siamese think it unlucky to pass under a rope on
which women's clothes are suspended. In New
Zealand the blood of women is supposed to have

* J. G. Frazer, quoting E. M. Curr.

disastrous effects upon males. If a South African
touches the blood of woman at certain periods his
bones become soft. If a woman steps over him,
or even over his spears he cannot hit his enemy
in battle. In Burmah it is an indignity to have
a woman overhead in a house of more than one
story, hence it is that most houses have but one
floor. In a house raised on piles, a servant will
not go in below the house for any purpose lest a
woman should be in the rooms over his head.

With divine and sacred persons a number of rules
have to be observed for their own safety and the
safety of the community. One of these is that the
sun may not shine upon them. The Mikado might
not touch the ground with his foot, nor was the sun
thought worthy to shine on his royal head. The heir
to the throne of Bogota forfeited his right to the succession if the sun shone direct upon him. In Sogomoso
the heir-apparent is shut up in seclusion for seven
years without seeing the light of the sun.* Now,
it is remarkable that girls at puberty and women
at regular intervals and after delivery are subjected
to the same rule of restrictions during a variable
period. In Laondo, a purely negro State, girls at
puberty are confined in separate huts, and may on
no account touch the ground during the period with
any part of their body. Among the Zulus and
kindred tribes, when the first signs of womanhood
show themselves, a girl, should she be walking or
working in the fields, runs to the river and hides herself for the day among the reeds that she may not be

* J. G. Frazer, quoting Alonzo de Zurita.

seen by men. Her head she covers with her blanket that the sun may not shine on it and shrivel her up into a withered skeleton, an assured result of any disregard of custom. At night she returns home and is closely secluded for a period of seven days. She then resumes her work. New Ireland girls are confined for four or five years in small cages and kept in the dark.*

Customs akin to these are world-wide, and have left in the folk-lore of all nations evidence of their being once universal. For example. A Greek story warns a princess to be careful in her fifteenth year lest the sun should shine on her. A Tyrolese legend tells how a lovely maiden was doomed to be transported to the belly of a whale, Jonah fashion, if ever a sunbeam fell upon her. Old Highland women, when I was a boy, always made a great ado if girls went, say to a hayfield, with bare heads. Boys might, but it was not good for girls. It was not altogether because they would get sunburned. There were "other things," all of which was conveyed to them in hints of Delphic ambiguity, but which was very awful to our youthful imagination.

The ground of this seclusion and guarding from sunlight lies in the dread primitive man has of woman's blood. Hence a woman must live apart during the period; she is then unclean, and, should any one come near her inadvertently, she must give them warning not to approach. Similar restrictions are imposed on women after delivery, when they are secluded and guarded for weeks. Nor are

---

[*] Rev. B. Banks.

restrictions confined to the periods referred to.
Precautions must be taken against accidents, as
these may happen at any moment. Scores of times
did I put the question to South Africans : "Why
do your women never enter the village by the paths
the men follow?" before I could get a satisfactory answer. I was told it was custom ; women
must be taught obedience ; people always did it ;
or that the master made rules and all must obey ;
that it was to keep wives from quarrelling if they
saw the head of the village walking frequently with
a favourite wife ; because men are greater, that is,
more sacred, than women ; " the woman is to a man
a child." Gradually and indirectly I came to know
that the restriction was designed to avoid accidents
such as might happen with the advent of womanhood unexpectedly. The object of all such restrictions
is to neutralise the dangerous influences which are
supposed to be connected with women at certain
periods. The woman is viewed as charged with
certain properties ; properties productive of evil in
themselves, and which, in certain circumstances, she
can use with infinite power for mischief. These
must be kept within bounds. If not, they may
prove destructive to the woman herself, as in the
Zulu shrivelling up, and to all with whom she comes
into contact.

The uncleanness of woman and the sanctity of the
sacred or divine man do not, to primitive men, differ
from one another. Both must be guarded against
and avoided when that is possible. Both must be
surrounded by taboos for this object as well as for

their own sakes, so that their properties, which are good or bad as they are directed, may be guided to be conducive of good to man.

Persons charged with such properties, and having at their disposal such powers for good or evil, cannot be without influence upon the community. Where every action has a supernatural significance, it is impossible to have any force in existence without its tending to give colour to all the institutions existing among men.

In a land where a woman may not touch a cow's udder* on pain of direst results, we may expect to find her wielding power however harshly she may be treated. Even from the most closely guarded harem come influences which go to make or mar the state. The Lubare of Uganda may be under the direction of a prophetess. In the Lake Region, the prophetess is all powerful, and may determine peace or war, as she often does in the south. The women of most African tribes are modest and retiring, and seldom address strangers except when they bring articles for sale, and even then it is not uncommon to find a husband or father accompany the woman to do the actual trading while she carries the burden. But this is not universal. There are tribes where the women are bold, aggressive and self-assertive. The Monbutto women are independent, obtrusive and immodest.† They do the field work as is done by all African women, but in other respects assert their independence in a manner rarely met with. The Monbutto are an island of humanity, in the very

* Felkin.   † Schweinfurth.

heart of Africa, differing in customs and habits from
all the surrounding tribes.　Their laws and observances resemble, and especially the aggressive immodesty of their women, those of certain minor
tribes inland from Inhambane more than that of any
other African people.　Dr. Schweinfurth does not
give in detail an account of their behaviour, but
leaves the reader to infer that as regards public
morality there is much to be desired.　Our information regarding the Inhambane tribes referred to is
also meagre.　A few years ago, a Lieut. Underwood
and a German missionary were travelling together
through the country.　Both were new to African
travel, and their ignorance of the language may
have prevented their understanding the meaning of
facts which came under their notice with painful
prominence.　So obtrusive did they find the women
that they were compelled to get some of their own
Swazi women camp-followers to mount guard over
their persons in their tents while they slept.*
Whether this was a natural aggressiveness of
character, or the ordinary courtesies of the country
I do not know.　It is common enough for a chief
to order one of the members of his harem to be
given to a distinguished stranger during his stay,
but the women will only repair to his tent at night
and as if by stealth.　Though not objecting to a
temporary change of husband, they cannot effect the
change during the day lest the gods should be
offended.†　When Dr. Felkin pressed King Mtesa
to replenish the mission larder, the king wearied

* Underwood, MS. notes.　　　　† Winterbotham.

with similar demands and anxious to settle the
question once for all, sent the doctor a parcel of
eighteen wives to attend upon him, and supply his
wants. The ungrateful man refused the kingly gift.

The subject of public morality it is impossible to
discuss in a popular work. But though not suitable
for the pages of a book intended for general readers,
its value in forming an estimate of the people's
character is considerable, and the man whose lot is
cast in Africa, cannot, without grave loss to his own
usefulness, dispense with an intimate acquaintance
with much that is unsavoury. To indicate the difficulty of dealing with this, I transcribe the first note
I made in collecting material for a separate chapter
on the subject. It is as follows:—" Before a Kordufan
girl consents to marry, she stipulates how many free
nights per week she may enjoy, and generally secures
every fourth night to do as she pleases." So
different are African standards from ours that
any thing said could only be suited for the pages of
a scientific journal, as is illustrated by the following
incident :—A missionary was one day addressing a
crowd of natives, many of whom had taken part in a
regular saturnalia held in the vicinity a few days
before. As he proceeded to denounce their customs
and their doings, I noticed a curious restlessness
among them. The climax was reached when he compared their behaviour, in search of drink and other
enjoyments, to that of strange dogs arriving at a
village, and sniffing about the places frequented by
local curs. To the natives this was not preaching ;
it was moral turpitude, and their feelings were tersely

expressed by an old chief, who, when outside, uttered the single word "filth," and walked away. The reason of this was plain. If there is one thing beyond all others against which the soul of an African rebels, it is to be compared to a dog, or to have it suggested that there can be anything in common between himself and his dog. A thief, it is true, is a wolf, but then thieves like wolves are made to be destroyed. So far is the aversion carried that there is a distinct "dog language," and the words composing it are never applied to men, except in defiance, or as the language of insult. To bid a man begone by the use of the word one applies to a dog, would be equivalent to throwing a glass of wine in a gentleman's eyes in the days when Irish steeple-chasing was in its glory. In a land where cowdung and urine are necessary requisites of the toilet, bury-ing a dog would prevent the growth of the season's crops.* It is by a knowledge of such customs and prejudices we can reach the minds of such peoples, and come to have an understanding of their domestic life. By beginning with what they can understand, we can gradually advance leading them to higher conceptions both of man and of God.

But while it is impossible to discuss the details of their moral code, there are broad outlines common to all primitive peoples which help us to an understand-ing of the progress of thought among them. The harem and zenana we may regard as a compara-tively late development ; the product of an advancing civilisation, and the growth of exclusive political

* Scillocks and Dinka.

power in the hands of the chief. The exclusiveness and sanctity of the harem could only be the product of settled government, permanent residence, and suitable buildings. Among a nation of hunters, wandering from place to place, a zenana would be an impossibility. Seclusion of any considerable number of persons would entail settled residence. At the same time, we find among primitive races that infidelity on the part of any of the king's wives is a capital offence, even if the custom is all but universal among the lower orders. To them a lapse on the part of a member of the royal household is a serious crime, while their opinion regarding other orders is faithfully expressed in the reply of the Kaffir to whom his missionary said, " I know many of you spend your nights roaming about after other men's wives." "No, master," he answered, "we do not do that, we have our own wives at night ; it is during the day our people go to see other women they love."* Another Scotch parson was asked, " How many wives have you," and on his replying that he had none, his interrogator asked sympathetically, "Was that because you could not get the cattle ? "

* Rev. J. Lundie, MS. notes.

CHAPTER XIII

A MORE savoury subject than public morality is courtesy, which in Africa is all that could be desired. Hospitality hardly knows any bounds, and the chief who receives a stranger as his guest treats him with courtesy and kindness. Many chiefs, on the great caravan routes, are now demoralised quite, and demand blackmail as one enters their territory, a demand sure to be repeated as he leaves. Man in the early days of the world regarded his neighbour as having a claim upon him, and in the age of hunting, food, while it lasted, was practically common property. To this day in times of great scarcity food is hardly ever stored up by families for their own use ; they share it with their more needy neighbours. They reason in this way :—The gods are good to men. They give them their food. They watch over the actions of their children, and as the fathers, who are now above, were good and kind to the stranger and the poor, it is their will that their children should obey custom. The whole of the past is wrapped in a halo of glory which myth weaves round it, and each man feels that he falls short of the ideal life if the stranger leaves his house hungry or empty-handed. When the native bards

sing the praises of the mighty dead, their deeds of
valour occupy a secondary place, as if that were
the necessary accompaniment of hospitality and the
courtesies of life to the hungry wayfarer.

The king, as the father of his people, is responsible
for village hospitality, and by a kind of fiscal ar-
rangement he levies a tax for this purpose on those
of his people best able to bear a burden. His acts
of kindness to strangers are representative acts, and
any failure on his part is a disgrace to the tribe.* I
remember once visiting a man of some local standing.
He sent me a fowl for my supper, and the councillor
who brought it seemed to be ashamed of his commission. Little was said, but I felt the reception I
met with did not promise success to my mission. I
was mistaken. After the clatter of tongues by the
camp fire ceased and all was still, the door of the hut
I occupied was cautiously opened, and the councillor
who had brought the fowl entered. In a low whisper
he said, "Here is meat," at the same time taking a
whole sheep's carcase from a young man who accompanied him. I asked what it meant; and the old
man's reply I shall never forget, "It is," he said
"nothing. You have bought it. Brandy has killed
my chief." Here was loyalty; loyalty to a chief whose
whole soul was in strong drink, to the neglect of all
the functions of royalty. He, as a councillor, could
not offer to do what his chief neglected, but his sense
of honour, and particularly the honour of his chief
and tribe, prompted him to do by stealth what he
felt was necessary to uphold ancient tradition, though

* J. Sutton, M.S. notes.

by doing it he put his neck in some danger. Very pathetic too were his words, " Brandy has killed my chief." The chief had not changed ; had not neglected the stranger ; did not forget the honour of his tribe. No. He was dead, that was all, and for his dead chief this loyal man did the courtesies of hospitality.

Philosophers and traditional theologians never weary of discussing the savage's moral sense and his innate ideas of right and wrong. They find it difficult to agree as to whether conscience is an inherent faculty, uniform in its manifestations among all classes and conditions of men, or an education of the moral sense which is capable of development according to man's stage of progress. I am not a philosopher nor a professed theologian. I am simply an observer of facts as these are met with every day in Savagedom. But as an observer I have often puzzled over the philosopher's right and wrong, and the ideas attached to these terms ; over his uniform manifestations, and the theologian's sweeping generalisations regarding all classes and conditions of men. I have wondered whether the philosopher's ideas of right and wrong are based on our Western conceptions—saturated as we have been by centuries of Christian ethics—of a well-ordered state and social system, or whether he would admit the Mosaic code as a correct expression of the innate ideas of right and wrong among the Jews at that time. And if so, whether conscience as such, apart from education, can have anything to say to such questions as arise about a plurality of wives, for example ? I have asked in vain if the traditional theologian would admit within the sphere of men acting according to their conscience, those who give their property, their subjects, and even their children to propitiate gods which to us are purely imaginary? Or whether we must regard them as wilfully violating the most sacred instincts of human nature in obedience to requirements which their sense of right and wrong calls vanity? Here again one asks, and asks in vain. No light is offered, or it is deeper than the mirk.

The one thing of which I am certain is this :— That these African races, whose religion we have been studying, not only profess their faith in its doctrines but really regulate their conduct by them, and that down to the minutest details of life. Their philosophy may be crude, but it is a philosophy. Nor is it altogether a false philosophy. It is the premises that are wrong, not the conclusion. It is their want of knowledge, not their lack of moral purpose. Their religion may be worse than none, but it is the form of it and the channels in which it runs which vitiate it, for the sincerity of the worshippers is infinitely more real than that of men who meet in Christian temples or worship God by proxy. The code of ethics practised by primitive man may shock our sensibilities, but he has reached it slowly, painfully, and prayerfully notwithstanding. To him religion is no pastime with which to amuse himself, but a matter of the most terrible reality ; a matter on which depends his present fortune and his future place among the ancestors. Does he bring his women to market ? He knows no better way, and must observe the prescribed rule for his own protection and theirs. Is his slain enemy's heart found in his broth pot ? This is not necessarily for love of human flesh, but to give him qualities which will ensure his own and his tribe's safety in war. Cannibalism I regard as a late development relatively ; a taste acquired in times of famine when men died like sheep and were devoured by their famished companions. This opinion I base on the partial distribution of the practice and its entire absence among most of the older races with which we have, in recent times, been brought into contact. For example :—

The Monbutto have no domestic animals, except dogs, and they are among the most pronounced cannibals in Africa. Such a people would suffer terribly if the crops failed even for a single season, and a succession of bad harvests would reduce them to actual starvation. What more natural than that this practice should have originated during a period of dire distress and want, and so became a national habit almost unconsciously. Stanley's forest cannibals seem, so far as we know, to depend entirely on vegetable substances for food. To them a few seasons of drought might mean extermination if they did not resort to human carrion. Abnormal developments do not belong to the ordinary progress of thought as I have attempted to trace it ; and the acts to which necessity has driven civilised men should warn us against hasty conclusions. Especially should it warn us against assuming that cannibalism was derived from any system of philosophy rather than from necessity and dire distress.

When primitive men walk abroad in nature's robes, and women adorn themselves with a tail of grass behind their backs as their sole garment after the manner of the Baris,* we are shocked at their immodesty, and cry out that they must be devoid of all sense of morality. This is exactly what a Monbutto mother would say to her daughter, if she appeared arrayed in the ample loin cloth worn by her brother rather than in her own bit of leaf attached lightly to her girdle. These are nature's own children doing nature's own bidding. They are advancing by steps so slow as to be imperceptible, by the same road by which our ancestors travelled thousands of years ago. They are at a stage of development now corresponding to that of the remote ancestors of the Ancient Greeks. To the primitive European, as to the primitive African, a simple code of morals was not only sufficient, it was complete, wise, and good ; the will of the gods. Only as he advanced did his moral perceptions grow, and so too will the primitive African's ; only let not the European expect too much, or look for permanent good on a large scale from a precocious and abnormal development of an individual here and there. Such individuals may do something within the sphere of their personal influence to raise their fellow countrymen. But only when new conceptions come to permeate the mass of the people, and the new philosophy commends itself as true for all classes, can

* Felkin.

there be a general upward movement. Such movements, when permanent, are by way of evolution
rather than revolution.

We are far from exhausting the religious aspect
of custom and myth when we have disposed of
public morals and the relation of the sexes. Religion
enters into the prosecution of the industrial arts and
even the amusements of life. The hunter has his
religious rites which he performs before he enters
the forest, and after he kills the first animal of the
chase. His return from a successful expedition must
be signalised by performing ceremonial acts. Even
the manner of carrying home the game is prescribed
by ritual.

When iron ore is dug and smelted, the smith
must observe certain rules and conform to the
necessary religious observances.* His forge must
be placed at a distance from the village dwellings,
and no one dare approach at the critical moment
when the molten metal begins to flow, except those
versed in the mysteries of the art. † The fire
used to cook first-fruits must not be kindled by a
vulgar brand snatched from the domestic hearth,
but must be sacred fire made by the magician in the
time-honoured way.‡ While the crops are growing
and before the feast of first-fruits is held, no forest
tree may be cut, as that would be to wound the
spirit of vegetation, which, to primitive man, would
be equivalent to wounding the god.

The sanctity of fire I have touched upon only
incidentally, but in connection with it there is an

* Myer, *Killimanjaro*.   † G. M. Theal.   ‡ J. Sutton, MS. notes.

elaborate ritual and endless restrictions. Fire as such is venerated. To kindle fire in an enemy's country during war is to invite sunshine and prosperity on one's foes. The sun is regarded as the father of fire. The moon too has her votaries and the devil dances of the Damaras are usually observed when the moon is full. So too the moon dances of West Africa, where their devil-houses are roofed with human skulls.* Dances before engaging in war are held during moonlight, and must not be neglected on pain of defeat and dire calamity. These and a thousand other minute observances enter into the daily religious life of the African, as they do into that of all primitive peoples. And the curious thing is, not that they resemble customs once common among civilised men, for the human mind in its search for knowledge works by the same methods in all lands, but that so much of what is ancient, dating back far beyond historic time, should survive among the nations of Europe.

A number of the observances referred to have been illustrated by survivals in civilised countries. These could be multiplied almost indefinitely. Even the Pondomise law forbidding the cutting of green wood while the crops are growing, has, or had recently, its corresponding custom in the remote Highlands of Scotland. I recollect hearing a Gaelic rhyme which enumerated the trees which might not be cut after " the opening of the leaf." The mountain ash, if to be used as a talisman, must be cut "while the leaf is in the bud." The willow must

* Waddell.

not be touched "after April day." I have no means of recovering the rhyme, but the woman who used to repeat it declared that in her younger days its directions were always observed by "wise people," but were now neglected by "a generation whose end was near." The worthy matron had the reputation of "knowing more than others."

Another custom which survived in Scotland till within the last seventy years, and which was doubtless a survival from very early times, was the Tein egin or forced fire. This was kindled on Mayday, and each villager, all domestic fires having been extinguished the previous evening, received a brand from the sacred pile with which to kindle their domestic hearths. Men who had failed to pay their debts, or had been guilty of notorious acts of meanness were refused the sacred fire, and this was equivalent to expulsion from one's club. It was for the time social ostracism. Nor were our Highlanders ignorant of trial by ordeal. They tied their witches hand and foot, after which they tossed them into a pond. If they floated they were taken out as the oracle proclaimed their innocence, but those of them who sank were allowed to drown. No farther trial was needed, for the ordeal never lied. So, too, the Felata of West Africa ascertains if the king's death was caused by his own wives by giving each member of the harem a dose of poison. These same Felata women, should they see the Juju or great fetish, when carried in procession, had such accidents as occasionally happen to pregnant mothers, and became sterile from that time. A similar fate happened to Highland women who saw the fairy bull. Blood brotherhood, which is so common in Africa, bears a close resemblance to foster brotherhood as between the heir to the chieftainship and the clansman with whom he was reared. But to enumerate more of such minor customs would be tedious. Their general tendency is all in one direction, and goes to show how slow is the process of evolution through which religious thought must pass before it reaches the higher conception of one supreme God, and the substitution of a single Incarnation, revealing the will of God to man, for the multitude of prophets who claim to hold converse with the unseen. From the ranks of these prophets, as the order recedes from its original ideal and purpose, men arise who strike into new paths and lead their fellows into the light of a higher conception of human life and the destiny that awaits humanity.

CHAPTER XIV

REFORMS

THE foregoing pages are but the barest outline of a subject of absorbing interest, not only to the ethnologist, but to all who wish to have an acquaintance with early processes of human thought. The facts are culled from the literature of Africa with occasional reference to the customs of other countries. These are few in number, and detached from their local setting, but they go to show that most of the customs that have survived must at one time have been common to the human family. From the days of the great dispersion, man has wandered hither and thither over the face of the earth, but he has never relaxed his hold of the few facts with which he started. To his little stock-in-trade of ideas he has clung with a tenacity only equalled by that with which he clung to life. He has added to his knowledge, adapted his ideas to new circumstances, discovered new facts and taken possession of them, but parted with nothing. This of itself shows how equally balanced his knowledge and his necessities must have been in the early days. He could part with nothing, and continue to exist till he had replaced it by something higher and better. The inventive faculty with which he was endowed

enabled him to widen his knowledge, and call to his
aid factors and forces which has made a gulf between
savage men and civilised which is almost, if not
altogether, absolute and impassable.

But is the gulf unfathomable, or even as deep as
it appears to many earnest students to be? Is
there not much common to both which seems to
bind them, over a long-forgotten past, into one
whole? May not the present gulf be bridged, and,
if bridged, how? By what means can civilised man
most easily and speedily bring within reach of his
savage brother's understanding those facts which
constitute the difference between them? How is primitive man to be persuaded that those forces which
civilised man calls to his aid are natural forces, con-
trolled by industrious application of what is ready
to any man's hand, rather than a more powerful
species of magic? Is it possible to convince an
African railway stoker that he is not generating
magic as he shovels coals into the fire-box? And,
if possible, how is it to be done?

"Supply him with blankets and flannel shirts,"
says one. In other words, extend European commerce to the remotest forest hut in Africa, and the
farthest headland of the northern seas, so that by a
mutual exchange of the African's ivory and gums,
and the Lapp's oil and tallow, for our manufactures,
they may, wearing our garments, be endowed with
our spirit. "Send him Bibles," says a second, and
make known to him the revealed Will of God.
You only demoralise him by your trade; he
ceases to be nature's nobleman, and he does not

become a creature of civilisation. Your trade and dress do not suit his condition ; his only hope is in being supplied with mental food and that food Divine truth." " Leave him to himself," says a third ; " he got on very well before the Bristol merchant found him out and plantations yearned for his presence among the sugar-canes. Besides, he made good progress in the interval until the Manchester spinner re-discovered him, and the Hamburg rum merchant began to pity his thirst." It is the old story of too many physicians. Like the Sick Man on the Bosphorus, every nation in Europe has a remedy, but the patient is seldom consulted, if at all.

The last class of physicians may be summarily dismissed. No man, if he be not a dreamer of impossible dreams, imagines it possible for one moment for civilised man to leave savage man alone. The inexorable evolution of events has brought them together after thousands of years of separation and wandering. Brothers still, re-united by a common destiny, they stand face to face, and on the races who know most, who can command agents to do their will, and who can calculate the probable currents of the future, will depend the fate of those who are still in the throes of the early struggles of the human mind. The cry out to leave savage man alone is but the language of ignorance or unchristian sloth. The apathy it implies is foreign to the healthy pulse of public opinion, and it may be left to the oblivion it deserves.

Of those who advocate commerce and industry apart from mental and moral training, or moral and religious instruction divorced from industry and commerce, each is earnest in the advocacy of the methods which appear to promise success, and believes that in the adoption of its theories a panacea would be found for all the ills that afflict savagedom. Make him work, says the latest gospel, and then he will come to feel his need of European commodities and luxuries. This will extend our commerce and benefit the savage, for then our business men and great capitalists will have an interest in him. These are not the exact words of introduction used by men preaching this gospel, but they express its purpose and meaning much more clearly than the approved definitions. I should be sorry if anything I may say should be construed against commercial enterprise and the introduction of a knowledge of the industrial arts into savage lands. On the contrary, I believe in both as powerful factors in the elevation of the human race, and that the spirit of persevering industry and trade, when it lays hold of a people, spurs them on towards both material and mental development. But it is well to look at the conditions fairly, and estimate things at their true value. The savage is nature's own child. He may have the cunning of the fox and the keenness of the lynx's eye when in his native forest, but bring him to a factory, and the glitter of a handful of glass beads fills his imagination with dreams of wealth. It may be that, being given to pombe, he asks for a stimulant. The principal articles of barter being trade rum and Holland square-face, he is treated to a drink of one of these, and tastes the fiery flavour.

He feels their prompt action, and from that day he is a doomed man. He has not the moral resolution to resist this demon of devil-water, which is more powerful than all his ancestral ghosts. In fact, he does not know the meaning of moral control against such a foe, and can see no good reason why he should not indulge in a daily carouse. He has sat by his chief's pombe-pot for hours and hours, and, beyond a slight drowsiness, felt no other ill-effects, and he does not understand why he should restrict himself to a limited measure of the drink provided by his friend the white man, whose commerce is to elevate him to take his place in the comity of nations. The evil is done, and the man who visits the factory adds one more life to the victims which must be slain that our commerce may extend, and an outlet be found for our surplus stock of bad spirits.

Nor is this all. The traffic that is carried on with drink as the medium of barter has far reaching effects beyond the moral deterioration of the native races. For rum a man will part with all he possesses, and the tribe where the trade is introduced is speedily reduced to beggary. This puts an end to profits, for there is nothing to exchange for our commodities. Where there was a roaring trade and men congratulated themselves on the advent of prosperous times, the fountains of supply suddenly dry up, and the only evidence of European influence left is moral ruin—this and a few blackened brick walls. It is the old nursery fable of the goose that laid the golden egg, only in Africa it is no fable but stern fact.

But ruin apart, and admitting trade to be carried

on in the most approved manner with useful goods
and ornamental articles, is savage man likely to be
improved by it to the extent the advocates of this
exclusive gospel of commerce seem to expect?
There is a distinct limit to the influence the glitter of
beads and even cotton loincloths have. The former
please only till they become common; the latter,
though an undoubted improvement upon bark cloth,
is but an indifferent substitute for a comfortable skin
garment, while it is less durable. As to industry
prospering to a large extent under present conditions, every man who knows Africa knows that is
impossible. To suppose that there is a moral virtue
in European garments, or in elaborate clothing of
any kind, as compared with a scanty covering of bark
cloth or skin, is to make the same mistake as was
made by the Government of the good King George,
when they concluded there must be a connection
between loyalty and breeches, and so put the Highlanders in trews by Act of Parliament.

So far as our knowledge of African peoples goes,
the kind and amount of clothing worn does not seem
to have any influence on public morals. The
Waganda clothe from head to foot, and put a man
to death if he walks about naked in a public place,
but their morality is very low, and offences against
the Seventh Commandment are common everywhere*. The Baris go almost naked, and they are
in no way noted for immodesty, but rather the
opposite. The Gowane are exceptionally well clad,
but this does not prevent their having a custom that

* Felkin.

a girl may not marry till she has borne a child. The paternity of this child is not inquired into. That is her own affair, and the husband has nothing to do with it. The child is sold as a slave. Among the Dyoor, with their scanty aprons, hardly equal to fig leaves, domestic affection is very marked, and the Bongo, who wear little clothing beyond a tail hanging down behind, limit their men to a maximum of three wives, a rare virtue in Africa.

It seems then that the gospel of cloth is not likely to raise the African to a perceptibly higher level than he is at present, if it be not accompanied by other influences more real and lasting, even if these cannot be measured out in fathoms or weighed by pounds avoirdupois.

And it is those other influences which in the ultimate result go to widen the market for European commodities, and to make the demand steady and sustained. Provinces which have been brought under a measure of Christian influence are our best customers. Every man who discards the savage life has wants which only civilised men can supply. These multiply as Christianity spreads, and when it has gained something more than toleration for itself, the influence it has upon the community is in proportion to the general appreciation of the changed conditions. The newly created wants develop new industries, and these go to build up the general prosperity of the community. This is not merely speculative opinion as to what we might expect, but a fact which has again and again been verified, and of which Basutoland is a conspicuous example.

But there is the great gospel of work. Teach the
African to work ; compel him to labour, and then
the products of his country will flow into our ware-
houses, iron and coffee, rubber and coal, copper and
cotton, nuts and oils, all valuable products which lie
ready to his hand if he would only believe the gospel—
of work. It is of no consequence that his wants are
few, and that he can supply them with little labour ;
that he neither knows our luxuries nor desires to
become acquainted with them. If he only takes
to labour as the love of his soul, all these things will
adjust themselves to our satisfaction and his own
benefit. His soil has the habit of yielding crops
with little labour and hardly any tillage, but this is
only the greater reason why he should be taught the
dignity of steady agricultural labour. And when
the land is barren ; where rain seldom falls and
crops cannot be grown except in a few favoured
spots—well, make him work ; give him a spade and
teach him to till the land. The sober truth is that
this gospel of work taken by itself is arrant nonsense.
Men must have a motive for work before they exert
themselves, and when that is present no people fail
to respond to the calls of duty. The Ancient
Greeks worked and that to some purpose, but they
were the most civilised people in the world, and
worked in response to the ideas which were current
among them. Englishmen work, and so do
Americans, but do Englishmen manufacture cloth
simply because they have the spinning and
weaving instinct ? Do they refrain from building baths such as the Romans built because the

architectural instinct is lying dormant? Do they
not manufacture because of an ulterior motive, the
accumulation of wealth? And are not our cities
without such baths as the Ancients had, simply
because we do not wash so often, and there is not
the same demand for them? These things we do,
and refrain from doing, not from any instincts or
love of work for its own sake, but because it suits
our purposes so to act.

So the African can and does work when there is
an adequate motive to spur him on. He can labour
for Europeans when such labour is within his reach,
and when he sees that he can procure what is of
value in his eyes with the product of his labour. He
can produce articles of commerce when these can
be disposed of to advantage. But suppose the
Waganda, in obedience to the call to work, produce
thousands of tons of surplus grain annually, will
their labour benefit either Europe or Africa? Certainly not. It will simply rot, and even Waganda
are not mad enough for that. Or, if Mr. Stanley's
pigmies collect ground-nuts by the ton ; what next?
Is each little man to walk a thousand miles, carrying three or four nuts, worth about a groat, to
market, and run the risk of being eaten for his
pains? Should the Baralongs produce iron to build
a fleet, what is to become of it? Or of the ships
should they build them? Lie on the stocks by the
edge of the forest waiting for a second Noah's
Deluge to float them? When we talk of the African
being taught to work, our ideas somehow run along
the coast line, and apply not so much to Africa as

such as to Africa in relation to our own commerce
and profit. We forget that we labour because powerful motives impel us, and that these motives are
within ; the result of thought, and our appreciation
of the true proportions of things. Such motives are
absent in Africa, and the intelligence to understand
as we do is absent. That we must first supply. I
once asked a steady and active farm-labourer if he
was fond of work, when the following colloquy took
place.

" I likes master weel enow, and tha'es geye guid
neeps."

"Yes," I replied ; " but do you like just to be
at work, because you do not want to sit at home ; to
get up in the morning and come out to the field."

" We's never axed, we hae our oors o' wark,"
was his laconic reply. No farther information was
to be had, so I bid my friend good morning, and
tried a group of women working in the next field
with even more disappointing results. Would
a nation of such men practise all the industrial
virtues the gospel of work expects, nay, demands in
the African ? Before men exert themselves in
industrial work they must realise that by such
means it is possible for them to advance in domestic
comfort, political importance, and national wealth.
And they must have an understanding that these
are desirable things to possess. In the case of the
African this last question is an important one. Does
he know or understand a condition of domestic
comfort higher than being allowed to live at peace
and cultivate his fields ? Do his ideas of political

importance go beyond his tribe being in a position
to make raids with safety and success upon his
neighbours ?   And as for national wealth, when that
consists of cattle liable to be stolen or driven away
wholesale before his very eyes, he is not likely to
exert himself, as is demanded of him, to increase their
number.   Only after a long preliminary training,
extending over several generations, will men living
in primitive simplicity understand the value of
labour as civilised men have learned to understand it.

Thought has always preceded material improve-
ments, and these have often come halting centuries
behind.   The man who gave birth to the new
thought saw his contemporaries despise his wisdom,
while they looked upon himself as a fanatic or mad-
man.   Seventy years ago it was proposed to fertilise
soil by means of electricity.   The project was turned
to ridicule by a practical farmer who described the
process as " muckin' the lan' wi' thunner."   It is
now admitted tardily that there was truth in the
thinker's idea, though he did not understand much
of the practical mysteries of " muckin' lan'."   At the
present day the gospel of work is to the African
simply " muckin' the lan' wi' thunner."

Another method for the elevation of the savage is
to send him the Bible, or in other words to preach to
him the doctrines of the various European Churches,
using the Bible as an authoritative text-book from
which there can be no appeal, and whose every
precept must be accepted once for all on pain of
Heaven's displeasure.   " Teach him," say they, " the

Word of God and leave it to work its own purposes. It is the leaven, the only leaven, that can affect for good the whole lump of heathenism." Let it be candidly admitted that such statements contain important truth. Let not the place occupied by Holy Scripture in the moral and spiritual elevation of mankind be minimised or disparaged. It is the only objective revelation of God we have, and the experience of two thousand years has shown it to be adapted to the needs of the human conscience. What philosophy failed to do has been done by the teaching of Jesus of Nazareth ; teaching at once so simple and sublime that no other has ever approached it. It stands unrivalled among all systems as He stands peerless among men. In any attempt made to raise men to a higher and purer life, the Gospel, in the full catholic sense, must ever be the chief factor. Without it civilisation lacks the most powerful of motives, and is apt to be but a thin veneer hiding unsightly rents and scars. But though the statement contains an important truth, it is not the whole truth. It is true, no doubt, we have the Apostles who preached the doctrines of the Gospel in their entirety, and insisted on an immediate and full acknowledgment of their lofty claim. Nor did they, to any considerable extent, insist on other branches of knowledge. These were, however, assumed. But with all this, few of their converts reached the ideal of the Christian life as the Apostles understood it, and as it is accepted in modern times.

Then the Apostles addressed, not primitive men

still in the shackles of barbarism, but the most
advanced and cultured peoples on the face of the
earth. The Jews had a unique history and
experiences, and the lofty morality taught by their
prophets put them in a position to understand, even
if they did not appreciate, apostolic doctrines and
the purity of life demanded by the teaching of the
founder of Christianity. They were widely scattered throughout the East. Their sacred books
were known everywhere, and thus the Apostles had
the nucleus of an attentive congregation wherever
they went. They invariably entered into the
Jewish synagogue on their arrival in a strange
town.

There they found an audience already familiar
with prophetic revelation, and eagerly waiting for
a farther development of it. No Jew regarded
Old Testament Scripture as having reached finality.
They were, besides, saturated with the civilisation of
the East. A long captivity made them familiar
with Babylonian astronomy. It gave them that
taste for trade and finance which is still characteristic of their race; an illustration of the persistency of ideas when once firmly rooted in the
national mind.

The influence of Jewish thought and literature
must have been considerable, and men in no way
friendly to Messianic hopes would be influenced by
it less or more. When a new form of religion was
presented to such men they would, in the first
case at least, give it a respectful hearing and carefully weigh its claims. The civilised habit of

thought current at the time would ensure a full
measure of discussion from the philosophical stand-
point. This gave it an undoubted advantage.
Truth seeks the light and courts discussion, and
the more the teaching and claims of Jesus were
subjected to criticism and discussed on their merits,
the wider would the sphere of His usefulness
become.

Then the Apostles made it their business to
thoroughly know the peoples they addressed.
Whether Jews, Greeks, Syrians, or Romans, the
early teachers of Christianity met them on their
own ground, and adapted their methods to suit
the peculiarities of each district or town. Their
writings clearly show that they made themselves
familiar with the thought, religion, and superstitions
of those they sought to influence, and when they
advanced the claims of their Master to universal
dominion over the hearts of men, it was to displace
beliefs the folly of which they were able to show.

Nor was this all. The Greeks, who ruled the
world of thought, were the most learned people in
the world. Poetry, art, sculpture and architecture
attained among them a degree of excellency which
has never been surpassed, while their philosophy
commands the admiration of the world after a lapse
of thousands of years. A philosophy which lives
still. Such were the people to whom the apostles
addressed the message they had for the world. A
people saturated with religious and philosophic
thought, and fully alive to all the advantages of
civilised habits of life.

Very different were those to whom Moses addressed his prophetic message when he went from Horeb to deliver them out of bondage. But even they were far removed from the stage at which the savage stands to-day. If they had lost the early traditions of their own race they were familiar with all that Egyptian religion and ritual could teach them, and knew what of civilisation the land of their sojourn contained. They were at that stage of development when new ideas would be seized upon, and held tenaciously by a large number, and so become in time part of the national thought. At an earlier period and in a ruder age, the father and founder of the Hebrew nation, moved by an impulse which struggled for expression, left his own country and became a wanderer in obedience to this conviction which he had. What thoughts of deity struggled within him and found expression in words seem to have been lost or forgotten by his descendants, till revived by Moses, whose ethical teaching during the early days of the wilderness journey was of the most elementary kind. "Hear, O Israel, the Lord our God is one God."

Round this central truth he grouped his doctrines and expanded their conceptions of deity. These were the spirituality of God; His purity and holiness. The cloud and the fire were the familiar emblems of his teaching. By such means did he lead their minds away from the Egyptian worship to a truer and higher conception of the One God.

Now to savage man these are absolutely new conceptions, but they are such as he can reach by way

of analogy and comparison.   His own ideas of public
and individual morality, on certain lines, help him,
and his conceptions of the spirits of greatly revered
ancestors lead up to an appreciation of the idea of a
holy, just, and upright God.   " The ancestors never
do wrong" is a cardinal article of African faith.
Beyond this he cannot travel unaided.   A man god
he can understand, and one may develop any day
under his very eyes.   A God man is beyond his
mental vision.   Nothing corresponding to this was
ever known to happen.   Nor did the Hebrews for
many a weary generation after the Exodus reach
the point at which we expect to find the savage
ready to join us.   It is true many embrace Christianity, and are in some respects patterns worthy of
our imitation, because they regulate their conduct by
the religion they profess, but as regards an intellectual understanding of, or an attempt at understanding, the conceptions of deity common in Europe,
few attain to that on first emerging from savage life
and the faith of millenniums.   The form of their
thought is something like this :—" The Lord Jesus
was holy, pure, sinless, good.   God loved him above
all other men.   The spirit of God was his, God dwelt
in him, and he speaks to us the words of God."   If in
this estimate of the conceptions of the Incarnation
by men emerging from the savage life, I can be shown
to be in error, no one will be better pleased than I
shall be myself.   That many native Christians can
glibly repeat our church formulas I am aware, and
the missionary who is content with that as an
evidence of an understanding of Christian doctrine is

a happy man.   He will burn with indignation at
native Christians being traduced, as he will feel
certain they are, by what has been said.   But if he
will take the trouble to occupy the same hut, with
half a dozen of his deacons or other office-bearers on
a Sunday night, and, pretending to be fast asleep,
listen to a discussion of his own sermon, he will
get a rude awakening.   The oftener he does this the
clearer will be his light if the greater his surprise.
By such means, and by casual questions to men off
their guard, did I learn what little I know of native
thought pure and unadulterated.   The results of my
experience I have faithfully portrayed so far as that
could be done in a few sentences.

Standing face to face with such facts the questions
which meet us on the threshold are not to be
answered in the airy manner suggested by those who
would send Bibles in countless thousands to savage
lands, or who would supply each man with a pick and
a mattock.   To make an impression on any people it
is necessary to reach down to their level of
thought, and become literally what St. Paul professed to be, "all things to all men."   If we are to
win primitive man to a higher and better life, or
in other words, if he is to escape extermination,
we must first of all know him.   It is said there is a
bit of the savage in every man, but this has been
covered over with so many layers of lacquer that
the child of the forest fails utterly to recognise as a
brother his civilised visitor.

When we have arrived at such knowledge of the
savage's thought as we can attain to, our next care

is to bring before his mind such conceptions as he can appreciate. The gulf between civilised man and savage is too great for the latter to realise at a bound, that it is possible for him to attain to all that the former has attained to. We, on the other hand, are so impatient of results that we expect the native to take kindly, in a single generation, to what it has taken us millenniums to reach. We forget how long it took the world to make a sewing-machine, and that we live in the age of Singers', while the African represents that of awls and sinews.

But if the first facts and truths presented to savage man must be simple, they must be none the less practical on that account. It is not necessary to denounce his customs as wrong and all wrong, for in point of fact they are not. There are certain facts and ideas common to all men, and these can be made the basis of instruction. For example. All natives regard theft as an evil and a crime; theft from a fellow tribesman, or superior being a special aggravation indicative of deepest depravity. So, too, are acts leading to war, arson, murder, and many more. Here we have something with which to begin. A moral foundation, based on a native philosophy, which all admit as true. But even here the savage has to learn much. It is wrong for a neighbouring tribe to cross the border and steal his cattle, but it somehow does not occur to primitive man that it is wrong for himself to cross that same border and steal his neighbour's cattle.

Passing from the moral code to conceptions of deity, we are on less solid ground, and opinions may differ as to the best methods to be followed. It seems to accord with reason that the same steps should be followed as in the moral code. One God, supreme, and omnipotent. Men responsible to Him, and their actions having a moral value are ideas which the savage can readily grasp. When we come to deal with the future, and the connection between this life and man's destiny, we are on less familiar ground, and primitive man is utterly at sea. The ideas are new, and nothing in his philosophy helps to explain them. The whole is a "white man's thing." The white man has, unfortunately, so many incomprehensible "things," some of them wise, some foolish, that this is apt to be the end of argument and of effort. If it is a "white man's thing," pure and simple, it is no use to try, for his magic is the more powerful. An intelligent and, I believe, truly pious man once said to me, "Master tells us to do, do; try again till we can be like the white man, we, or our grandchildren. How can that be? I heard my missionary say many times we are the race of Ham, and in the Bible a curse was upon them. That curse is on us. That is why we are not like the white men. It is no use to try." These were his exact words, and if they prove nothing else they prove this:—That ethnology is not a suitable study for primitive man, nor for some missionaries. Perhaps, it is not suitable for public preaching to civilised man or savage. It may prove too much or too little.

With the growth of thought, when new ideas become common property, primitive men will move forward with the progress of the world. The progress should now be much more rapid than when the Greek mind worked its way to a philosophy which still lives. The results and experience of the past affords an immense leverage, and what we need is, that the Christian thought of the Western world, and with it, the ideas of life, private and national which are consistent with such thought, should be presented to the savage mind in the form most attractive to men, and as they advance the dawn of a new intelligence will come with the opening up of a new world of thought and work. As new ideals fill the mind, the old will be displaced and forgotten, as has already happened to systems which crumbled under their own weight. The traces of these vanished systems carry us back to a period so remote, and conceptions so simple, that the philosophy of the Africa of to-day is an advanced system compared to it.

Much of this work will fall to the lot of the Christian Church, and on her wisdom, and the prudence and practical sagacity of her agents, the progress of the native races largely depends. Ethnology may not be a suitable study for savage man, but he who would teach his primitive brother can have no better mental equipment than a thorough understanding of the processes by which nations develop, and the paths that have in the past led to progress. The Church that first adopts for her intending missionaries the study of Comparative Religion as a substitute for subjects now taught, will lead the van in the path of true progress in that department of Christian work which has in it the greatest possibilities for the future of the world. It will save the missionary years of comparatively useless labour in the discovery of facts for himself, and from the first bring him into touch with the thought of savage men.

INDEX